BEYOND STYLE

Other books by Gary Provost:

The Dorchester Gas Tank
Make Every Word Count
The Freelance Writer's Handbook
The Pork Chop War
100 Ways to Improve Your Writing
Good If It Goes (co-authored with Gail Provost)
Fatal Dosage
Popcorn (co-authored with Gail Provost)
Finder (co-authored with Marilyn Greene)
David & Max (co-authored with Gail Provost)

BEYOND STYLE

Mastering the Finer Points of Writing

GARY PROVOST

Writer's
Digest
Books

Cincinnati, Ohio

91 90 89   5 4 3 2

Library of Congress Cataloging-in-Publication Data

Provost, Gary, 1944-
    Beyond style/Gary Provost.
    p. cm.
    Includes index.
    ISBN 0-89879-314-9
    1. Authorship.   I. Title.
PN145.P68   1988
808'.02—dc19   87-34082
                                                                   CIP

Design by Joan Jacobus

I want to gratefully acknowledge permission to reprint the following material:

Excerpt from *The Great Gatsby* by F. Scott Fitzgerald. Copyright © 1926 Charles Scribner's Sons; copyright renewed 1953 Frances Scott Fitzgerald Lanahan. Reprinted with the permission of Charles Scribner's Sons (Macmillan Company).

Excerpt from *The Collected Stories Of Isaac Bashevis Singer*. Copyright © 1953; copyright renewed 1981, 1982 by Isaac Bashevis Singer. Reprinted with the permission of Farrar, Straus and Giroux.

Excerpt from *A Catskill Eagle* by Robert B. Parker. Copyright © 1985 by Robert Parker. Reprinted with the permission of Delacorte Press.

Excerpt from *Children Of Light* by Robert Stone. Copyright © 1985, 1986 Robert Stone. Reprinted with the permission of Alfred A. Knopf, Inc.

In June of 1987 I ran my first Writer's Retreat Workshop at Senexet House in Woodstock, Connecticut. In order to make the WRW a success I had to find thirteen writers who were willing to spend their money, give up their time, abandon their jobs and families for a while, and bring their writing hopes to Woodstock, all in the faith that I could help them grow as writers. Thanks to their commitment to their work, their good humor, and their talents, the workshop was a big success, we all grew as writers, and I had the most satisfying teaching experience of my career. And so this book is fondly dedicated to the members of the first graduating class of the Writer's Retreat Workshop:

Carolyn Biehler, Rick Brigham, Rachel Cann, Jody Halsted, Maria Kohler, Jeff Levin, Gary Lines, Rea Martin, Milada Marsalka, Russ Rideout, Marcy Sakofsky, Ted Schlaegel, Guy Vallee.

Contents

Acknowledgments

Some of the material in this book appeared in different form in *Writer's Digest* magazine. I want to thank Bill Brohaugh and Tom Clark at Writer's Digest for their work on the original articles.

At Writer's Digest Books I want to thank Carol Cartaino, Jean Fredette, and especially, Sharon Rudd, who did such wonderful work in editing the book.

Thanks also to the many writers whose good work I have used as examples in this book:

Woody Allen, Cleveland Amory, Christopher P. Andersen, Saul Bellow, Stanley Bing, Phillip Bingham, Michael Blowen, William Faulkner, William Goldman, Elizabeth Loftus, Gregory McDonald, Gabriel Garcia Marquez, Edwin O'Connor, Erich Segal, Scott Spencer, Douglas Wallop, and Denise Worrell.

And a special thanks to those writer-friends and friendly writers who shared with me some of their work, time, and knowledge:

Jim Bellarosa, Anne Bernays, Lou Burnett, Phyllis Feurstein, Gary Goshgarian, Ellen Goodman, Ted Groff, Christopher Hewitt, Crosby Holden, Bonnie Ireland, Trish Janeshutz, Justin Kaplan, Christopher Keane, Ken Lizotte, Steve Lowe, Joe McGinniss, Marie Melville, Robert Parker, Gail Provost, Bob Reiss, Ruth Rosing, and Dan Wakefield.

And finally, special thanks to Evan Marshall.

Introduction

In 1980 Writer's Digest Books published my first book, *Make Every Word Count*. It was a writing technique book for beginning writers. In retrospect, it seems a little presumptuous to think that my first book was about how to write well. But what the heck, the book is in its third printing, and eight years after it came out I am still very proud of it, which is more than I can say for some of the things I wrote fifteen years ago.

When I wrote *Make Every Word Count* I was getting published in local newspapers, small literary magazines, and regional and national magazines. But back then I still thought of getting published as difficult.

The most important thing I've learned since then is getting published is easy. Writing well is what's hard.

And why shouldn't it be? You are, after all, trying to make a reader believe in a dream. With a scattering of black lines on white paper you are trying to convince him that movie stars and professional athletes are in the room with him talking about their work, that a voice is instructing him in the finer points of cooking chicken, that a pirate ship is on the horizon, that two hesitant lovers are finally kissing, that a space ship from the planet Zo is about to land.

Of course it's hard. You have nothing to work with but words and the unpredictable mind of a reader you have never met.

Just because every bozo you meet in the grocery store tells you, "Yeah, I'm thinking of writing a book myself," doesn't mean that writing is easy. Where is his book? Have you read it? No, because he discovered one rainy night that writing was harder than giving blood, that he had not the vaguest idea of even how to begin.

Maybe you're not getting published as often as you would like. Maybe you're not getting published at all. There's a good reason. It's because writing well is so damned hard that your writing may not yet be good enough. If you can accept that fact, then you will probably succeed as a writer. If you resist it, if you blame your rejections on moronic editors, narrow-minded publishers, and a public that just doesn't understand what you are trying to say, then your failure is as certain as tomorrow's sunrise. You must have humility about your work. It is the only thing that can save you.

I know what I'm talking about. When I was in my twenties I wrote seven wretched books that I thought were destined for best-sellerdom. I sent each to about thirty publishers and collected enough rejection slips to wallpaper a medium-sized garage. And each time a manuscript came back I thought, "My God, this editor is an idiot!" I was astounded at the number of fools who were allowed to sit in editorial offices. Not only that, but somebody was letting these idiots read my short stories and articles, too, because those were also being rejected.

Now I'm smarter. I know a lot more about good writing and I know that constant rejection means only one thing: the writing isn't good enough. It was true for me then, and it's true for you now.

Why is that so hard for us to accept? One reason is that our writing is so personal. When someone says our writing is not good, they pierce the skin. It feels as if they have come very close to saying *we* are no good. People used to tell me things that were wrong with my stories and I would go cold and stony on them. Of course, when I got home I'd make the changes, but still, I was hurt. That's human nature. The other reason we have trouble accepting the fact that our writing isn't good enough is much simpler. It looks great to us. And hell, we ought to know. We wrote it.

That is at once the cruelest and the kindest thing about writing. The cruelty is that we can write something that's quite atrocious, and if we are new to the craft it will look wonderful to us. We all think our baby is beautiful. No wonder we're shocked when it is spurned. I've written a lot of stories that I thought were fabulous, and now I know they were best used as kitty litter. I can guarantee that if you are getting rejected regularly the pages you wrote today will make you want to vomit next year.

The kindness, of course, is that the delusion that our writing is good writing is the thing that keeps us going until the writing really is good.

Please write this on a piece of paper and tape it over your desk: IF I AM NOT WRITING WELL ENOUGH TO GET PUBLISHED, THEN I AM NOT QUALIFIED TO JUDGE THE MERIT OF MY OWN WORK.

An introduction in a book like this is supposed to be inspirational. It's supposed to make you feel good about your writing, enthusiastic, hopeful. And by now you're probably wondering, "What the hell kind of inspiration is this, Gary, telling me that writing well is hard and that my writing is lousy?"

But think about it. If I told you that your writing is fine, but that the peculiarities of editors and other machinations of the publishing world had conspired to leave you out, I would be telling you that there is no hope. Your fate would not be in your hands. But I'm telling you that constant rejection means you are not writing well enough yet, and that means that you have control of the situation. You, not them. All you have to do is work harder and study more and keep an open mind about your writing. Be persistent, be humble, and be curious, and your writing dreams will come true. I know this for a fact, and that's why I wrote this book.

Since *Make Every Word Count* I have sold one category romance novel, four novels for children, one book on the business of being a freelance writer, one writing book for a general audience, one nonfiction sports book, two true crime dramas, and two movies. During that time I have also published hundreds of magazine articles, short stories, newspaper columns, and even two poems. I have won the National Jewish Book Award without being Jewish, and I came close to being the new Ann Landers without being a woman. For ten years in my twenties I couldn't get a word published and now writing dreams come true for me every day.

I still don't know all there is to know about writing. I still make mistakes. I'm still learning.

But I have grown. So have the readers of *Make Every Word Count*. And so have you.

I wanted to write a book about writing fiction and nonfiction that reflects growth, that goes beyond *Make Every Word Count,* beyond style, beyond the work you can do in sentences, and into the soul of good writing.

Make Every Word Count is largely about things you can see—active verbs, clichés, character tags, etc. It includes points of writing technique that can be isolated in words or sentences, the kind of thing I can point to and say "take this out" or "put this in." *Beyond Style* contains many of those points, but primarily it is about things you can't see because they are not located on any one line or page in the manuscript. *Beyond Style* is about invisible things like the relationship between form and content; proportion and pacing; slant and theme; plot tension and surface tension; how to keep the reader under the reading spell; how to orchestrate the sound of your writing.

You don't have to read *Make Every Word Count* or any other writing book before you read this. While I have written this book with a slightly advanced audience in mind, I have tried to ground all my discussions in language and ideas that will make the beginner comfortable. For that reason some of what I wrote in *Make Every Word Count* and some of the things you have read in other books will be repeated here.

Every chapter in this book is for writers of fiction and nonfiction. There is nothing here that should be discarded by the writer who works exclusively in one form or the other. The best fiction writers of the past have influenced the greatest journalists of our time, and they in turn are influencing the new writers of fiction. Increasingly, the difference between nonfiction and fiction is one of content, not of form or technique. So read the book with your own projects in mind, whether they are fiction or nonfiction, but read all of it.

The book is in three sections. In Section One, chapters on Style, Pace, Unity, Sound, and Imagery will show you how to make the reading experience pleasant and easy. But a reader won't stick with a story just because it is easy to read. It must also be compelling, and in Section Two we will discuss the qualities that make a piece of reading compelling, in chapters on Originality, Credibility, Subtlety, and Tension.

And finally, after you have learned to make the reading experience easy, pleasant, and compelling, you want to maintain consistency, you want to avoid shattering the reader's reading dream. We will discuss that in chapters on Viewpoint and Form. Between the sections I have inserted "coffee breaks," during which we will discuss Identification and Time.

You'll find that many of the points made in one chapter could just as well be made in another, and sometimes they will be. That's because writing is an art, not a science, and it can never be sliced into even pieces.

In this book you will find what I have learned about good writing. My teachers have been my own mistakes, occasional editors who have been kind enough to set me straight, and my students. In 1986 I offered a manuscript criticism service by mail. In 1987 I started my Writer's Retreat Workshops. People often ask me why I do these things. One reason is that I learn more about writing by critiquing manuscripts and teaching at my workshops than I ever would have learned in college if I had gone.

You, too, will learn from some of my students. Several of them have generously allowed me to publish excerpts from their work. I am particularly proud of the students (ranging in age, incidentally, from twenty to seventy-nine) whose work appears here. The nature of this book requires that in most cases I show you not the things they are doing right, but something they did wrong. Surely having your mistakes discussed in public is no more fun than having a tooth filled. But the willingness to have his manuscript held up for constructive criticism is often the difference between a writer whose work ends up in print and the writer whose work ends up in the attic.

I've tried not to write an introduction that says "Writing is easy; all you have to do is follow the advice in this book." That would be dishonest. I've told you how very hard writing is because it is. But I haven't told you this to discourage you. I've told you to encourage you. Because if you're frustrated with your writing, if you're growing pessimistic, if you are sometimes visited with despair as I was—that sickening feeling that you could write forever and never get published—then perhaps it is because you thought learning to write well was going to be easy. Now that you know how very, very hard it is, you can see how well you are really doing. I can't promise that writing will get any easier, but I do promise that after you read this book your writing will be much better.

So these are the finer points of writing, and after you have mastered them you will see things in your work that are invisible now. You will see mistakes in every old manuscript, and opportunities in every new one.

PART
ONE

Style

If you've never read a book on style, you can still read this book and nothing bad will happen. But my assumption with this book is that the reader has done a good deal of writing, and perhaps published some of it. He or she may have taken a few writing courses, and has probably read some books about writing style, such as *The Elements of Style,* or basic writing books that have large sections on style, such as *Make Every Word Count*. So in this book I am not going to spend many pages on the rules of style.

However, everything about writing bears repeating, so this section is a brief course in style for those who have not been exposed to it, and a refresher for those who have.

What Style Is

Style is not what you write, but how you write it. Style is the form, not the content. The following sentences all have the same content, the same information, but they have different styles.

It could not be used.

It was useless.

It failed to function.

Junk, pure junk!

It was as useless as a rule book at a riot.

So what's the right style? All of them. Voltaire said, "Every style that is not boring is a good one."

Rules of Style

The rules of style are not like the rules of arithmetic. Nobody can prove that one way is better than another. But there are valid generalizations about which writing techniques create the most interesting, most compelling reading, and when those generalizations can be applied to individual sentences, they are called "rules of style." No rule of style should be followed 100 percent of the time. Writing is an art, not a science, and there are many times in your writing when the "wrong" way is the right way because of the context, or the mood you are trying to create. But a fair guideline is this: Always obey the rule of style unless you know why you think the writing works better some other way.

Avoid Wordiness

This has two meanings. It means avoid using more words than you need. Don't write "In terms of my education I got a diploma from Resnikoff College, which I graduated from on June 10 in the spring of 1964." Write "I graduated from Resnikoff College on June 10, 1964."

"Avoid wordiness" also means don't use long, abstract, unfamiliar words when you can use simple, concrete, common words. In other words, don't write like a lawyer. Don't write "Herewith enclosed for your consideration are the instruments of liability waiver made mandatory by the requirement that we eschew any litigation contingencies." Write "Here are the releases we have to sign so we won't get sued." When you write, reach for the rhythms of spoken language. Reading your words should be as easy as listening to an articulate speaker.

Show, Don't Tell

This is the only rule of style that often requires you to use more words, not fewer, so you cannot practice it all the time. "Show, don't tell" means don't give the reader words when you can give her pictures. Don't write "Todd's movement was very fast," when you can write "Todd ran like a fox."

Use the Active Voice

The active voice means that the subject of a sentence is doing the action of the sentence. "The house was surrounded by Major Garonovitch and his helpers" is a passive-voice sentence. "Major Garonovitch and his helpers surrounded the house" is an active-voice sentence.

Say Things in a Positive Way

If you write about two teenagers exploring a quarry who come upon a cave and you write, "There was no light in the cave," the first thing the reader will see is the light that's not there. You are writing in a negative way; you are telling the reader what is not true. But if you write in a positive way, "The cave was dark," you communicate to the reader what you are really trying to show him: darkness.

Be Specific

If I tell you that a dog attacked me when I was coming home from the Food World today, you get a vague picture about a general dog. If I tell you specifically, "A poodle attacked me," you can see my scene much more clearly.

Use Strong Verbs

Don't use vague verbs that are boosted by adverbs. Don't write, "The senator ate quickly," if you can write "the senator gobbled," or "The senator wolfed."

Don't use weak general verbs like *walk, cry, fall,* and *touch* if the situation calls for *plod, weep, collapse,* and *caress.*

Don't Reach for Style

If a style of writing doesn't come easily to you, then it's probably not coming easily to the reader either. Style is not something that you add to the subject matter like adding water to cake mix. Style is embedded in the material. It can't be poured in or sifted out.

Don't try to write your piece on dog collars "like Erma Bombeck," or your short story "like Ernest Hemingway." Style must come from who you are, not who you wish you were. Just relax and write as well as you can. Style will take care of itself.

Style Is Simplicity

Here are the beginnings of three novels:

> The book of ballads published by Von Humboldt Fleisher in the Thirties was an immediate hit. Humboldt was just what everyone had been waiting for. Out in the Midwest I had certainly been waiting eagerly, I can tell you that. An avant-garde writer, the first of a new generation, he was handsome, fair, large, serious, witty, he was learned. This guy had it all.

> I wasn't born yet so it was Cousin Gowan who was there and big enough to see and remember and tell me afterward when I was big enough for it to make sense. That is, it was Cousin Gowan plus Uncle Gavin or maybe Uncle Gavin rather plus Cousin Gowan. He—Cousin Gowan—was thirteen. His grandfather was Grandfather's brother, so by the time it got down to us, he and I didn't know what cousin to each other we were. So he just called all of us except Grandfather "cousin" and all of us except Grandfather called him "cousin" and let it go at that.

> On the day they were going to kill him, Santiago Nasar got up at five-thirty in the morning to wait for the boat the bishop was coming on. He'd dreamed he was going through a grove of timber trees where a gentle drizzle was falling, and for an instant he was happy in his dream, but when he awoke he felt completely spattered with bird shit.

Consider those three paragraphs. Look at the style. Are they weighted with symbolism? Are they lined with beautiful metaphors?

Are they knotted into great and complex poetry? Are they deep? Do they mean so much that they must be read three times to be understood?

No. They are all simple, direct, unpretentious. The style in each is unadorned, and every sentence is like an arrow aimed at exactly what it means to say. Each author is trying to do just one thing, tell a story.

The three paragraphs are the work of Nobel Prize winners. The first is from *Humboldt's Gift,* by Saul Bellow, the second from *The Town,* by William Faulkner, and the last from *Chronicle of a Death Foretold,* by Gabriel Garcia Marquez.

Now you know the secret of good writing style. And you also know how to get to Stockholm.

Style Is Everything

There are many other rules of style, but these are the ones that have to be respected in almost every paragraph that you write. Many other rules of style concern punctuation and grammar, which are not the province of this book. And I'm ignoring several other rules of style here, such as "work from a suitable design," because they will be covered when we discuss larger subjects like unity and subtlety.

I said that in this book I wouldn't spend many pages on the rules of style. But in a larger sense everything in this book, and all other writing technique books, is about style. Martin Amis said, "Style is everything and nothing. It is not that, as is commonly supposed, you get your content and soup it up with style; style is absolutely embedded in the way you perceive."

Pace

The paperback dictionary I always keep within arm's reach says that *pace* means "the rate of movement or progress." As we discuss it here, I am thinking about the overall pace of your article, story, or book. But I'm also thinking about the pace of that story at any given sentence or paragraph. A few slow passages in an otherwise fast-moving story can be as distressing to a reader as a few long traffic jams in an otherwise fast trip. So along with pace, we'll be talking about proportion and balance, and avoiding traffic jams.

Luggage

When an editor says, "I hate the pace of your story," or words to that effect, he sometimes means that the pace is too fast, or it's inconsistent and jarring. But 90 percent of the time he means the pace is too slow. The story drags. It's boring.

Your story has got to move fast. But that doesn't mean that you have to mount your reader on a rocket and hurl her through space. A nice leisurely horse and carriage ride can also be pleasant. "Keep the story moving" means that your story should always feel as if it is moving with maximum efficiency. If it's a horse and a carriage ride, fine, but don't make it feel as if the horse is near death and the wheels are square.

It's all a matter of luggage. Yes, luggage. If you don't believe me, just walk down the street with two loaded suitcases in your hands, then walk down the street without them. Luggage can slow down any vehicle, whether it's a horse-drawn carriage or a Ferrari. So what are you going to do, drive to Pennsylvania without any clean shirts? No. You're going to drive to Pennsylvania without your tool kit and your silverware and all the other things you don't need in Pennsylvania. In order to make your story move at maximum efficiency you must get rid of the excess luggage.

Rich description, detailed characterization, and extended dialogue are not necessarily excess luggage. They can be very valuable luggage and you don't want to toss them out on the highway just for the sake of a faster pace. What you do want to jettison is the luggage you don't need. Throw away that rusty old baby carriage that you jammed into the trunk even though the last baby is already in college. Get rid of that leaden bowling ball that you haven't rolled since Gerald Ford was president. And abandon once and for all that garish purple and green thing that Uncle Charlie gave you three Christmases ago. You're never going to use it; you don't even know what it is. We're talking junk here, ugly, heavy, worthless junk. That's what makes cars sluggish, and that's what makes stories sluggish.

I find junk in all of the manuscripts I read, including my own first drafts.

Most of the junk comes in the form of unnecessary words. By this point in your career, you've probably read and heard a lot about unnecessary words, so I'll be brief.

A word is unnecessary if it is not doing any work, if it's doing work that doesn't have to be done, or if it's doing work that's being done by other nearby words.

To come up with a few examples I've looked into a manuscript sent to me by Arlene Scott. Arlene was at the beginning of her writing career, and she sent me a novel called *Love Lost*. This happens to be fiction, but the mistakes are just as common in nonfiction. I was impressed by Arlene's sense of storytelling, and just the fact that she had completed a novel made me optimistic about her writing future. But like many of the writers I hear from, she had created a story that could be compared to a sleek and beautiful racing car that had been buried under so much junk that it could hardly move faster than forty miles an hour. In critiquing her I told her to shovel away all that junk, so that her readers could enjoy a fast ride in her beautiful car.

I told Arlene to be on the lookout for words and phrases that took up space but didn't bring any new information.

Compare:

But for some reason today there was only a handful of shoppers.

with:

Today there was only a handful of shoppers.

The phrase "but for some reason" is meaningless. It doesn't tell the reader anything she doesn't already know.

At one point Arlene had her heroine, Linda, go to the liquor cabinet and pour a stiff drink into a glass "from one of the bottles." That phrase was doing no work. Of course the drink was from one of the bottles.

Arlene also tended to use diluters like *almost* a lot.

She wrote "A whiff of expensive perfume almost got Linda's attention for a moment as she moved slowly . . ."

Well, the whiff must have gotten Linda's attention or she wouldn't know that it was expensive or even that it was there.

Later Arlene wrote, "It almost seemed as if he timed his visits to his father when he knew he wouldn't be home."

Arlene didn't mean "It almost seemed." She meant "It seemed." You can catch these kinds of unnecessary words by looking more carefully at what you've written and thinking about what it says.

Like many new writers, Arlene also tended to create unnecessary luggage by using passive language. Many writers, for example, write something like "John was able to climb the drain pipe and sneak into Elena's bedroom," instead of "John climbed the drain pipe and sneaked into Elena's bedroom." Don't say that somebody was able to do something when you mean to say that he did it.

Each of these words and phrases that Arlene yanked from her story weighs about as much as a quarter-inch nail. Not very heavy. But try filling the back seat of your car with sacks of quarter-inch nails and see how fast you go.

I've given you just a few examples of unnecessary words that can keep your story from running at maximum efficiency. You can probably think of hundreds of others. If not, you should review the discussions of unnecessary words in books that are primarily about style, such as *Make Every Word Count* (Writer's Digest Books), *100 Ways to Improve Your Writing* (New American Library) and the excellent *Getting the Words Right: How to Revise, Edit and Rewrite,* by Theodore Cheney (Writer's Digest Books). We'll also talk more about this in the chapter on "Subtlety."

The Lead

You must get your story off to a good start. Editors will not read through several slow pages to see if things pick up later. The first few paragraphs are the most important. That's when the reader decides if he's going to stay for the ride. You must set a fast pace as soon as the starting gun is fired. Remember, this doesn't mean you have to go at breakneck speed. It means you must move with maximum efficiency while carrying all the luggage that's *necessary* for your particular story. You must write a good lead.

Many writers make the reader feel as if she is at the bottom of a steep hill, by beginning with background. Many college professors, despite the fact that they are unable to write a single coherent sentence, set out to write biographies, and the first thing they do is bludgeon the reader into boredom with long and intricate explanations of who was married to whom and which immigrant Scottish sheepherder fathered the girl who would marry the man whose daughter would become the mother of the fellow the book is about . . . zzz. A lot of novice novelists do the same thing.

I discussed this tiresome practice with Justin Kaplan, one of the nation's top biographers. Kaplan, who won the Pulitzer Prize and the National Book Award for *Mr. Clemens and Mark Twain,* said, "All that genealogical stuff bores the crap out of me. I mean if you don't even know a person to begin with, how are you going to keep his grandparents straight? A lot of biographies are just plain abysmal."

What's abysmal in biographies is abysmal in all other writing. Kaplan might as well have said, "If you don't even care about a person to begin with, why would you want to keep his grandparents straight?"

Make the reader care.

That's how you get your story off at a fast pace.

When I wrote an article on the Solcotrans blood bag for *Family Circle* magazine, I could have begun with a lot of background information, explaining what the bag was, when it was developed, etc. But I knew my reader would be carried along by my story if I got him involved first, if I wrote a lead that made him care about my subject. I began:

> Do you ever worry that someday you might need an operation and there won't be enough blood in the blood bank to save you? Or it will turn out that you have some rare blood type, difficult to replace? Or you'll get contaminated blood?
>
> I do. Everybody does.
>
> These are nasty little fears, but they are not unrealistic in the age of AIDS. Blood supplies are diminishing all over the country because donors believe, incorrectly, that they can get AIDS from giving blood. And people who are going to receive blood have a higher rate of anxiety, fearing that they will get contaminated blood.
>
> But what if you didn't have to depend on other people's blood? What if you could have transfusions of the best blood of all? Your own.
>
> You can.

Now here is a very different lead. It's one of my favorites, the first paragraph from Scott Spencer's novel *Endless Love*.

> When I was seventeen and in full obedience to my heart's most urgent commands, I stepped far from the pathway of normal life and in a moment's time ruined everything I loved—I loved so deeply, and when the love was interrupted, when the incorporeal body of love shrank back in terror and my own body was locked away, it was hard for others to believe that a life so new could suffer so irrevocably. But now, years have passed and the night of August 12, 1967, still divides my life.

That lead does what a lead should do. It makes the reader care and it makes him ask questions. What on earth could the narrator have done at age seventeen? The narrator says, in effect, "I did something bad and I was punished." The author makes you care enough so that you want to stick around and find out exactly what happened. Another reason that I like the lead is that it is a little bit old-fashioned; it has the comforting quality of a fairy tale or the pirate tales we read as children. I think there is an instant of loneliness just before we pick up a book, and we're looking for an author to say, "Here I am, and I'm going to tell you a story." Spencer does that with the very first sentence.

Even though that paragraph from *Endless Love* is a good example of a fictional lead, there is something far more important that I want you to see in it, and that's why I'm going to use it again in a little while.

Make Things Happen

A fast pace means that something happens, then something else happens, and then another thing happens. Things just keep happening. There should be no long passages during which nothing happens. Even the horse-drawn carriage keeps moving; it doesn't stop. Putting it another way, if nothing is happening, why are you writing about it? You don't come home from work and describe to your spouse all the moments during the day when nothing was happening.

Three years ago a friend of mine named Steve Lowe gave me a section of manuscript from his novel in progress, *Aurora*. I took the pages home and read them, but I didn't have to read many to tell Steve why his manuscript would be rejected. Here is a passage:

> Sunrise began to paint its kaleidoscope of pastels on the desert of New Mexico. The cool August morning gave way rapidly to rising temperatures and to the gray-violet outline of butte and cactus. These forms, hidden for hours in darkness, now appeared in changing hues of pink and orange. Step by step, the sun's palette distributed its gentle splendor onto a vast canvas of stillness.
>
> All night long the man-made glare of white light shone from massive staging platforms and block-shaped buildings that made up Section IV of Holloman Air Force Base. The strong white dots from these lamps now became less and less intense as the sun set to work establishing its light and warmth over all of the base's 160 square miles. When the sun showed its full shimmering roundness on the eastern horizon, the white lights faded in intensity and surrendered their usefulness. Observing this regular changing of the guard on the flat expanse below, the night's fingernail moon shone brilliantly against its borrowed setting of fragile indigo. It, too, began to fade, in obedience to the sun's powerful daily magic.

I used to write like that. Everybody used to write like that. We all begin as youthful writers no matter how old we are when first we write, and we are filled to the brim with poetic ways of describing things, especially sunsets and girls we yearn for. Desperate to impress, and convinced that we are clever, we write passages that have no pace at all. From the first word to the last, the reader has not moved an inch. Nothing has happened. It's all description.

Description is the thing that makes what's happening more vivid; description should never be the thing that's happening.

When you write anything, don't "get around" to the people and the action. Put them right on every page in every paragraph. Description is worthless if the reader doesn't care about the thing being described. Nobody cares if "Sunrise began to paint its kaleidoscope of pastels on the desert" unless there is on that desert some person they can identify with. Now be honest, do you really care what the weather is like in New Mexico right now? Probably not, unless you are in New Mexico, or have friends there. Well, of course I said all of this to Steve Lowe. And the next time I saw him he had rewritten the book seven times and sold it to Dodd, Mead, which published it in hardcover. It was later reprinted in paperback by Gold Eagle Books. This is how it starts.

A mixture of snow squalls and chilling rain churned its way from the sharp peaks of the Canadian Rockies and whirled southward to Evergreen, Colorado. Institute Director Dennis Covino watched the storm, seeking solace in the September swirl of gray and white. Darts of rain pecked at the wall-sized window, making him edgy yet grateful; at least it gave him an excuse to turn his attention away from his animated guest. He palmed the desktop, turning toward the fat man, William Hendley of Hendley International Industries, who waved home another point, grabbing at the air above his bald head like a magician preparing a finale. Let it be the finale, the director thought. Wind it up, please God, wind it up.

"Make no mistake, Doctor," Hendley continued. "The other side is still years—I might say light years—ahead of us in celestial research, and you know it. This project will send chills down their spines. Like the moon landing. We get there first. It'll freeze them in their tracks. We are needed, both of us, to keep the other side honest."

Covino nodded. "The other side," he thought. Never "the Reds" or "the Russians," just "the other side." Devils versus angels.

In the passage I gave you from the unpublishable version of *Aurora,* nobody did anything. In this passage from the published novel, there is only one sentence in which nobody is doing anything. Pace is people doing things, things happening, and the more things that happen on a given page, the faster the pace.

So what about nonfiction? Can "things happen" in nonfiction: can "people do things" in an article about, say, "The Smells of Boston"?

Sure. Just by coincidence I happen to have written an article on that very subject, and here are a few paragraphs from it.

Haymarket Square, the revived Quincy Market, the North End, all meld into one great bazaar of street vendors, flea markets, open air cafes, restaurants, and most of all, food. If you are thinking in particular of food shopping, waltz over to Haymarket, where pandemonium reigns every Saturday. Muttons and beeves hang in little downstairs shops here, and the air is thick with the essence of everything from apples to zucchini pyramided in creaking pushcarts. Every item is peddled by howling merchants who are as much show biz as food biz. And besides, where else can you get a pound of asparagus for 79 cents?

If, on the other hand, raw sides of beef don't do much for you, try the Market or the North End. Walking through Quincy Market is enough to boggle even the most discriminating nose. Let your nasal passages point the way—you may end up tracking down just-baked chocolate chip cookies at the Boston Chipyard, fresh, crusty french bread at Au Bon Pain, or even fettucine Alfredo at Cricket's restaurant.

True, those paragraphs are about foods that smell good, but people are waltzing to Haymarket square, muttons are hanging in shops, items are being peddled, merchants are howling, noses are being boggled, cookies are being tracked down, and a character named "you" is sniffing his way all over town. Things are definitely happening.

All of which brings us back to Scott Spencer and that first paragraph from *Endless Love.*

Many times when I tell a student that a page or several pages in his manuscript have to be cremated because they have no signs of life, he tells me that he reads lots of published books like that. "What about James Michener?" he says.

It's true that a few successful authors write pages of description that move with all the speed of a slug worm and get them published, either because their prose is so unusually compelling or their reputation is so lofty that the reader knows his persistence will be rewarded. But usually when a new writer thinks he has read published work that is as static as his own, it is an illusion. He is mimicking what he thinks he read, but a closer inspection will show him that there's a lot more going on in the published work. Scott Spencer is a fine example. Here, again, is the first paragraph from *Endless Love*.

> When I was seventeen and in full obedience to my heart's most urgent commands, I stepped far from the pathway of normal life and in a moment's time ruined everything I loved—I loved so deeply, and when the love was interrupted, when the incorporeal body of love shrank back in terror and my own body was locked away, it was hard for others to believe that a life so new could suffer so irrevocably. But now, years have passed and the night of August 12, 1967, still divides my life.

Spencer is using a rich and somewhat passive style here and it would be easy for the reader to imagine that she had read some lovely prose but not much "story." The illusion is that the pace is slow and the prose still satisfying.

But just how slow is the pace? How much really happens in that paragraph? Well, a kid steps away from a pathway, then he ruins everything he loves, he loves deeply, then some love gets interrupted, and a body shrinks back, then another body gets locked away, and others can't believe something, and a life suffers, and then years pass, and a night divides.

All that in just ninety words.

Look at your own writing. Listen to it. Ask yourself: Are things happening or are they just being? If they are just being, the pace is not fast enough.

Keep Pace with Quotes

Quote is really the verb, and *quotation* is the noun, but everybody uses *quote* as a noun as in "Did you get some good quotes when you interviewed Pia Zadora's uncle?" So I will, too.

The main thing I want to say about quotes is: use them. Good quotes used in the right place will keep your article moving.

"The most common mistake I see among writers of nonficton is that they don't use quotes. Without quotes, the writing moves too slowly," an editor once told me. "If I don't see several quotes in an article I will reject it."

Let that be a lesson to you.

Of course, there are many lively published articles that have no quotes in them, but usually they are short. Most articles written without quotes are as slow as sludge; the only thing fast about them is the speed with which they are rejected by editors. If you can quote the man on the street, the expert on your subject, or the person you are writing about, you will usually make your article livelier, faster paced, and more salable.

Some Examples

There's a book called *The Book of People* by Christopher P. Andersen, (Perigee). It's a collection of profiles of celebrities. With each profile Andersen has isolated one quote so that you can taste the flavor of that celebrity. Andersen has a composer's ear for a good quote. His selections are excellent. Get this book and read all the quotes. Then you'll know what a good quote is. Here are some of them. Note that these quotes don't just provide information; they reveal something about the character of the speaker.

> *"I really wanted to be an adventurer, to lay pipeline in South America or be a cabin boy, but I didn't have the guts."* —Edward Asner

> *"I've learned to get angry enough to tell people to go to hell, which you've got to do. Getting out of my shell was my biggest problem."* —Richard Chamberlain

> *"I think it's neat that a lot of people are still making money off my mother. Bone-picking was never my bag."* —Liza Minelli

When to Quote

There are no absolute rules about where you should sprinkle quotes to give your articles a steady and lively pace, but here are some guidelines:

1. When you haven't quoted for several paragraphs and the page is starting to look like one big block of print.

2. When you want to reveal something about the speaker's character.
3. When the speaker has said something in a way that is funnier, more colorful, more succinct, or just generally more interesting than the way you might cover the same information.

Compare

Eydie Gorme says she doesn't like most of the music of recent years. She feels that the lyrics are asinine and ridiculous and that radio stations have very low standards.

with

"I think the music of the last fifteen years is horrendous," she says, "I can't stand the ridiculous, asinine lyrics coming out of human beings' throats. Radio stations insist on playing computerized crap."

4. When the information is a lot more significant because of who is saying it.

Compare

Donahue is sure that flying saucers will land in Elgin, Illinois, sometime next July, and that an army of bite-sized Saturnites will imprison that town for the next twelve years.

with

"Flying saucers will land in Elgin, Illinois, next July. I'm not guessing. I know," says Walt Donahue, Director of President Reagan's commission on extraterrestrial life forms. Mr. Donahue, generally regarded as the nation's most informed and respected UFO researcher, says, "I've got proof that an army of bite-sized Saturnites plans to imprison Elgin for the next twelve years."

5. When the material has emotional, not just informational, content. If a woman says, "I have a son," don't quote her. If she says, "I love my son," or "I hate my son," or "My son has a drug problem and I feel so helpless," then quote her.

Don't Describe Quotes

When you quote a person, don't slow the pace by taking time to describe the quote as having been "exclaimed" or "uttered" or "opined."

" 'I think the country is in a dreadful mess,' she opined," doesn't do any more work than " 'I think the country is in a dreadful mess,' she said."

The second sentence moves faster because there is no reader resistance to the simple word *said* whereas *opined* takes an extra second to process.

There are times when you will get some added meaning from an "exclaimed," or an "announced," but generally the quote should contain its own tone of voice.

Don't Repeat Information in Quotes

When I first became a newspaper reporter I had a bad habit of stating something, and then repeating it in quotes. I often wrote things like this:

> Mayor Keane told the City Council last night that he will not support the bond issue for a new recreation center.

> "I've decided not to support the bond issue for a new recreation center," Keane told the council. "If we don't have the cash on hand for a new recreation center, then that's tough cookies," he said.

If a runner had to run every yard twice like that, you can see that it would slow his pace. So don't do it.

Balance the Quotes

What's the right amount of butter to put on an ear of corn? Whatever it takes to make the corn taste best. Nobody can tell you the exact amount, but we can all agree that a pound is too much and a pinch is too little.

It's the same thing with quotes. Work for a balance that is pleasing to the eye and to the ear.

I have in front of me an article called "Meet a James Garner You'll Hardly Recognize," by Mary Murphy (*TV Guide,* Dec. 13, 1986). Let's see, paragraph by paragraph, how Mary balanced her quoted and non-quoted material. Keep in mind that a profile like this would normally have a lot more quotes than, say, an article about the talking frogs of Ecuador.

1. No quotes.
2. No quotes.

3. Half quotes.
4. All quotes.
5. All quotes.
6. All quotes.
7. No quotes.
8. No quotes.
9. Half quotes.
10. About two-thirds quotes.
11. No quotes
12. Half quotes.
13. No quotes.
14. Half quotes.
15. No quotes.
16. About 10 percent quotes.
17. No quotes.
18. No quotes.
19. All quotes.
20. No quotes.

There are fifteen more paragraphs, but you get the idea. Notice that Mary never writes more than three paragraphs of quotes in a row, or more than two paragraphs in a row without quotes. I'm not saying you should adopt that particular formula, but it does give you an example of a nice balance that creates a pleasing pace.

Trim the Quotes

If you quote every word a man or woman said, you will burden your article with tons of unnecessary luggage. Speakers are wordy. They are always speaking in the first draft. Remember, you are aiming for maximum efficiency. That means getting the most work out of the fewest words, which includes quotes. Don't change the speaker's meaning. Just throw away the words you don't need.

Your expert may say: "I've got a lot of market research in my desk. You wouldn't believe how many reports I read in a week. They come from universities, corporations, consumer groups, you name it. All of it points to one thing. By 1990 we'll be paying more to insure the safety of products than we will for the products themselves." But you should write: "All of the research points to one thing. By 1990 we'll be paying more to insure the safety of products than we will for the products themselves."

Variety

When you use quotes, remember it is their *difference* that makes them interesting. An article that is all quotes could be as boring as one that has none. Quotes can speed up the pace of an article or nonfiction book by adding a variety of sights and sounds for the reader to look at and listen to. It is that *variety* that makes the trip go faster. When you look out the window of a jet airliner you don't have much sense of the speed because everything looks the same. Bringing it down to earth, a ten-hour drive through New England would not seem to take as long as a ten-hour drive across Texas.

Pace Nonfiction with Dialogue

We usually think of dialogue as something we put into our short stories and novels, but if quotes can quicken the pace of nonfiction, dialogue should be able to do the same thing. And it can. My last two books were nonfiction and both of them have as much dialogue as the average novel. Without dialogue both of them would have been boring.

Here's an example of how I used dialogue in *Fatal Dosage*. Anne Capute was a nurse accused of a mercy killing. On her first meeting with her lawyer she implied that there had been other mercy killings at the same hospital. I could have summarized that meeting and explained the implications of what was said, but it would have been like slashing a tire on a moving car. With dialogue I could make the story move faster. I wrote:

"Are you sure the doctor said she's only got twenty-four to forty-eight hours to live?" Pat asked.

"Yes," Anne said. "I'm sure about that. Is it okay to smoke in here?"

Pat glanced at Don Harwood and Beth Whitehead to see if they objected. Neither did. "Sure, go ahead," he said. He didn't like smoking, but he wanted a happy client.

Anne lit a cigarette and stretched her legs in front of her. She was feeling more comfortable now. "Yes," she said, "Norma was definitely a prime candidate for the celestial air force."

Pat was reaching into a lower desk drawer for an ashtray, and he froze suddenly, as if someone had struck him.

"The celestial air force?" he said. He sat up and grabbed his pen.

"Yes," Anne said, "that's what we called it. We used to joke about helping a terminal patient to join the celestial air force."

"Who?"

"The nurses."

Pat was stunned. "Are you telling me this sort of thing went on before?"

"Well, I don't think anybody was turning out a body a week," Anne said. "But . . ." Now Anne leaned forward for the first time and looked Pat straight in the eye. "Look," she said, "you have to understand about nurses."

Of course the events of *Fatal Dosage* are easy to relate in traditional storytelling fashion, so the material cries out for dialogue. But a magazine or newspaper article is usually not a narrative with a beginning and an ending. Because of this, and because you must economize on words, you can't use a lot of dialogue in most articles. But in many articles you will find that a small amount of dialogue can be used and it can improve the pace of the story by giving life to people on the page, breaking up the page visually, and creating a new sound for the reader to listen to. That's what Stanley Bing did in his article about good management techniques (*Esquire*, April 1986).

"I'm wondering how such a dumb thing could happen to such a smart bunch of people," Don mused at the meeting dedicated to sorting out the crisis. He smoothed his translucent pate for a fearful moment, then chortled. "I'll tell you what," he said. "Let's forget about pointing fingers and try to see how the best staff in the business can make sure this kind of thing doesn't happen again. Okay, gang?"

When Should You Use Dialogue?

With nonfiction, dialogue is sometimes useful, but with fiction it is essential for a pleasing pace. Your short stories will sail with dialogue, and often sink without it. And if you write a novel with little or no dialogue, chances are no editor will ever get anywhere near the end of it. Well-written dialogue used in the right places is, for many readers, the best part of the reading experience.

Many writers are not comfortable writing dialogue, so they never use it. Other writers are too comfortable writing dialogue, so they use it when they shouldn't. I can't give you a precise formula for when to use dialogue and when not to, but I can give you a pretty good guideline.

As you begin any sentence, or any paragraph, there is a job you are trying to get done. Think about what that job is and ask yourself, "Who can do that job best: dialogue or narrative?"

Here are some examples of jobs you might need done, and how your two workers might do them.

1. *PROVIDE INFORMATION.*

   Narrative: It had been three years since Ralph had seen Carol.

   Dialogue: "It's been three years since I've seen Carol," Ralph said.

2. *REVEAL CHARACTER.*

   Narrative: Angela had a violent temper.

   Dialogue: "So help me," Angela shrieked, "if you ask me that one more time I'm going to smack your face, and I mean hard."

3. *MOVE THE STORY FORWARD.*

   Narrative: When Talbot got to the warehouse he realized that Vinnie had murdered Markowitz.

   Dialogue: "Freeze, Talbot, or I'll give you what I gave your sleazy friend, Markowitz."

4. *CREATE A SENSE OF PLACE.*

   Narrative: Beauregard invited his friends to return.

   Dialogue: "Y'all come back real soon, you heah."

Here are some other jobs you might want done. See if you can come up with examples of how dialogue and narrative might do them:

5. CREATE A SENSE OF TIME, SUCH AS THE MIDDLE AGES.

6. DESCRIBE A PLACE.

7. SUMMARIZE MUCH OF WHAT HAS ALREADY HAPPENED.

"Okay, Gary, that's great," you're thinking. "I'll just use whatever does the best job in any situation. But how do you define 'best job,' bozo?"

You can't define it exactly. But you can get a pretty good idea by asking yourself several questions.

Which way will accomplish the most work for the number of words spent? Which way will excite my reader? Which way is in contrast to what has been going on for the last several paragraphs? (If you've just written two pages of dialogue, then the answer is narrative.) Which way is most pleasing to the reader's eye? Is this material I want to focus on or is it just transitional material getting me from one point in my story to another?

After you have asked yourself these questions, and read the advice about dialogue in other parts of this book, go with your instincts. But remember, you're looking for the *best* way, not the *easiest* way. So ask yourself one more question: "Am I writing it this way because I don't have confidence in my ability to write it the other way?"

Don't Write Unnecessary Dialogue

While good dialogue can improve the pace of your story, keep in mind that unnecessary dialogue is just a bunch of unnecessary words with quote marks around them.

Dialogue should never be used to fill up space on the page, to create scenes when a simple transition will do, or to cover ground that could be covered more quickly or effectively with narrative.

Just because something can be put in dialogue doesn't mean it should be. If it has no story value, character value, or information value, it won't improve the pace of your story, so don't put it in dialogue.

One of the mistakes I see often in manuscripts is the creation of dialogue for introductions.

"Jeff, I'd like you to meet Mrs. Heffner," Angie said. I reached out and shook Mrs. Heffner's hand.

"Hi, Jeff," she said, smiling.

"And this young lady is Mrs. Heffner's secretary, Deanna Frost," Angie said. "Deanna, this is Jeff Conti."

We shook hands. "Hi, Deanna."

"Hi," she said. "Nice to meet you."

Some writers do this every time one character is introduced to another. It's boring. It makes the story crawl. It frustrates the reader. Just write: "Angie introduced me to Mrs. Heffner and Deanna Frost, her secretary."

Then get on with it.

There is no unsinkable rule about when you should use dialogue and when you shouldn't. But here's a good generalization: Look at the dialogue you have written and ask yourself, "If a stranger were nearby would she try to eavesdrop on this conversation?" If the answer is no, don't use dialogue. If the answer is yes, use it.

Proportion

I said earlier that things shouldn't just *be* in your stories; things should happen.

But how often?

That question perplexes many writers. How often should something happen? Ned walks into a room and you want to say a few things about Ned before Ned does something. But how many things should you say about Ned? Should you tell the reader everything that Ned is wearing? Should you tell the reader where Ned was born? How much can you tell before something else should happen?

What are the proportions?

It would be lovely if there were a magic formula I could give you. But then writing wouldn't be art anymore; it would be some weird thing that's done the same way by all the people who know the magic formula. So I can't. But we can do some exploring together.

Your story is made up of what we'll call "story events" and "additional information." The story events are the things that happen, that make it a story, the things you say when you're telling somebody about the story. Like this:

"See, this guy named Joe is in jail for a couple of days for vagrancy and he overhears another guy talking about a robbery he pulled off and how the cops never found the cash, because he has such a clever hiding place. So Joe figures that this guy is just dying to boast about his clever hiding place if he can find someone who won't go and steal the money. So Joe pretends that's he's in for murder and will probably be in prison for life, and he flatters the guy and the guy reveals the hiding place. So when Joe gets out two days later he goes to get the money, only the dead body of the guy's wife is also there and Joe gets sick and runs away."

Additional information is the description, the details, the background.

The pace of your story is set by the number of story events. The more story events you have per page, the faster the pace of the story. If every sentence were a story event, the thing would fly by, but it wouldn't really be a story. It would be a summary, like the one about Joe.

The additional information is as necessary to your story as costumes, sets and lights are to a stage show. But if the story events are continually interrupted by thirty lines of description,. detail, and background, the story will be a flop. How long would you sit and look at an empty stage, or one on which the actors are just standing around doing nothing?

Very few intermediate writers are setting too fast a pace. Almost all of them are moving too slowly. Almost all of them put in too much description, detail, and background. Or, putting it another way: junk. They don't know when to stop.

So let's compare a typical unpublished manuscript with a typical published one.

Ted is a Florida writer who sent me a 100,000-word novel called *At the End of the Killing*. He's got a lot of talent, a good eye, and terrific story sense. His story is in excellent shape these days, but when he sent it to me it moved slower than a check from a publisher, which, believe me, moves pretty slowly. "Dear Ted," I wrote. "You have sent me a good 50,000-word novel. Unfortunately, you have smothered it to death under another 50,000 unnecessary words."

Ted laughs about his overwriting now, but I don't think he was amused when I told him to cut 50,000 words out of his novel.

Here are 600 or so words of the novel as Ted originally sent it to me. I will italicize the story events. Everything else is additional information.

Dan ran his eyes down the street, then across the street to the apartment buildings nestled in the gloom. He would not know which building to enter until he crossed the street and checked the numbers.

Cold wind swept a paper bag past his feet, then over his shadow, made full by the insipid rays of the street lamp above him. He stepped back to the corner of the building, to kill the shadow, to still the biting wind.

Above the buildings he could see the incandescent splendor of a thousand stars—twinkling and glistening, they appeared to him as brilliant white diamonds clinging to invisible fingers. Diamonds reminded him of words from a Beatles' song his daughter used to sing around the house: Lucy in the Sky with Diamonds. She said the words implied an LSD trip. *The box in his hand made Dan wonder about the trip he was on.* Delivering a package at ten o'clock was absurd. But Peter had insisted on it, saying the man would not be home until this hour.

Dan studied the buildings again. He would cross the street where he stood and hug the buildings for warmth while searching for the address. It was a freak cold wave cutting its way through Miami on this last day in March. The weatherman had promised that it would break by noon tomorrow.

Eerie light danced and swirled in the cavern of air space between the rows of facing apartment buildings, the product of a fierce but futile battle for supremacy being waged by the half moon and the street lamps. Under this eerie light the street lay brooding. The street gave it off as though it were shimmering heat produced by the blinding midday sun. The brooding of the street lapped over the sidewalk and touched Dan's feet.

Far away the urgent scream of a police siren rent the night air. Dan stomped his feet to warm them, then told himself to relax. The Machiavellian effect of the street was only an illusion, given the late hour and the cold. He turned his watch to the street lamp and noticed that six minutes yet remained until the hour of ten. He would cut the minutes in half and then cross the street.

He thought of Peter, how noticeably Peter had aged in the four months since they had last played golf together, the bags under his eyes darker, more pronounced, a new furrow creeping from the corner of his left eye toward his cheekbone. *Responding to a call from Peter, he had arrived in Peter's office at three in the afternoon,* surprised to find Peter less than his usual effervescent self. *Peter had wasted little time addressing the purpose of his phone call, the box resting on the edge of his desk. Would Dan Curtiss be so kind as to deliver the box?*

In the first paragraph Dan is standing on the street with a package in his hand. Seven paragraphs later he is still there. That would be okay if those seven paragraphs were filled with story events in flashback or in Dan's memory. But they are not. They are filled with the streetlights, the weather, etc. Ted could quicken the pace of this material by deleting everything but what I italicized.

Dan ran his eyes down the street, then across the street to the apartment buildings nestled in the gloom. The box in his hand made Dan wonder about the trip he was on.

Responding to a call from Peter, he had arrived in Peter's office at three in the afternoon. Peter had wasted little time in addressing the purpose of his phone call, the box resting on the edge of his desk. Would Dan Curtiss be so kind as to deliver the box?

Can you hear the difference in the pace? The second version is at top speed. You certainly don't have to write everything like that, but keep in mind that your reader is reading to see what happens next, not about lights, brooding streets, and weather, etc.

Now here's the first six hundred words from published material of the same type, Robert Parker's best-selling Spenser novel *A Catskill Eagle* (Delacorte). Again, I'll italicize the story events.

It was nearly midnight and I was just getting home from detecting. I had followed an embezzler around on a warm day in early summer trying to observe him spending his ill-gotten gain. The best I'd been able to do was catch him eating a veal cutlet sandwich in a sub shop in Danvers Square across from Security National Bank. It wasn't much, but it was as close as you could get to sin in Danvers. *I got a Steinlager from the refrigerator and opened it and sat at the counter to read my mail. There was* a check from a client, a consumer protection letter from the phone company, a threat of a field collection from the electric company, *and a letter from Susan.*

The letter said:

I have no time. Hawk is in jail in Mill River, California. You must get him out. I need help too. Hawk will explain. Things are awful, but I love you.

Susan

And no matter how many times I read it, *that's all it said. It was postmarked San Jose.*

I drank some beer. A drop of condensation made a shimmery track down the side of the green bottle. Steinlager, New Zealand, the label said. Probably some corruption between the Dutch Zeeland and the English Sealand. Language worked funny. *I got off the stool very carefully and went slowly and got my atlas and looked up Mill River, California. It was south of San Francisco.* Population 10,753. I drank another swallow of beer. *Then I went to the phone and dialed. Vince Haller answered on the fifth ring.* I said it was me.

He said, "Jesus Christ, it's twenty minutes of one."

I said, "Hawk's in jail in a small town called Mill River south of San Francisco. *I want you to get a lawyer in there now.*"

"At twenty minutes of fucking one?" Haller said.

"Susan's in trouble, too. *I'm going out in the morning. I want to hear from the lawyer before I go.*"

"What kind of trouble?" Haller said.

"I don't know. Hawk knows. *Get the lawyer down there right now.*"

"*Okay, I'll call a firm we know in San Francisco. They can roust one of their junior partners out and send him down,* it's only about quarter of ten out there."

"*I want to hear from him as soon as he's seen Hawk.*"

Haller said, "You okay?"

I said, "Get going, Vince," and hung up.

I got another beer and read Susan's letter again. It said the same thing. I sat at the counter beside the phone and looked at my apartment.

Bookcases on either side of the front window. A working fireplace. Living room, bedroom, kitchen and bath. A shotgun, a rifle, and three handguns.

"I've been here too long," I said. I didn't like the way I sounded in the empty room. I got up and walked to the front window and looked down at Marlborough Street. Nothing was happening down there. I went back to the counter and drank some beer. Good to keep busy.

The phone rang at four twelve in the morning. My second bottle of beer had gone flat on the counter, half finished, and I was lying on my back on the couch with my hands behind my head, looking at my ceiling. *I answered the phone,* before the third ring.

At the other end, a woman's voice said, "Mr. Spenser?"

I said yes.

She said, "This is Paula Goldman. I'm an attorney with Stein, Faye, and Corbett in San Francisco and I was asked to call you."

As you can see, Parker doesn't allow too much additional information to get between story events. He keeps things moving. There are a lot of story events there, and I didn't even italicize the ones we're hearing for the second time. Parker doesn't stop to describe the curtains and couches in Spenser's apartment, he doesn't tell us how Spenser met Susan, or who exactly Hawk is. He puts us in the car and starts driving at a pretty good clip. He will drive us by everything he wants us to see, but you'd better bring a sandwich because he won't stop anywhere for lunch.

If this particular passage were written down as a paragraph-by-paragraph formula showing the proportion of "story event" sentences to "additional information" sentences, it would look like this:

Event. Event. Info. Info.

Event. Event.

Event.

Event. Event. Event. Event. Event. Event.

Event.

Info. Info. Info. Info. Info. Info. Event. Event. Info. Info. Event. Event. Info.

Info.

Event. Event.

Info.

Info. Event.

Info.

Info. Event.

Event.

Event.

Info.

Info.

Info. Info. Info.

Info. Info. Info. Info.

Event. Info. Info. Info. Info.

Event. Info. Event.

Event.

Event.

Event. Event.

As you can see, there are only two paragraphs that have more than one sentence and no story events.

I've used a published detective novel here to show fast pace because it was an unpublished detective novel that I used to show slow pace. Keep in mind that a detective novel like *A Catskill Eagle* is usually faster paced than the average novel. I haven't put this here as a formula for you to follow. It is just an example for you to measure yourself against. Take something that you have written and write the formula the way I have with Parker. Your proportions of events to additional material don't have to be the same as Parker's, but they should be a lot closer to that than to the example I gave you earlier.

A good pace means that the reader can hear the author saying, "this happened and then that happened and then this happened and then that happened and then. . . ."

Story Events in Nonfiction

A work of nonfiction has as many story events as a work of fiction. The difference is that the story events in nonfiction don't add up to a plot;

they add up to a body of information. But the generalizations about pace still apply. Keep those story events coming.

The most obvious story events in nonfiction would be anecdotes, which are complete little stories, and the events in a narrative like "The Day I Met the Pope."

But most nonfiction story events don't come in such neat little packages. When you are writing articles about the mating habits of mice, or high-tech medical diagnostic tools, most of your story events are sentences or phrases that are like a series of illustrative snapshots that you flash before the reader. These snapshots would be a hodge-podge in a work of fiction, but in nonfiction the rules are different. The story events don't have to build suspense, reveal character, etc. They just have to make an orderly contribution to the collection of information.

Here's an example:

A bottle of milk breaks, and then a guy gets through life, but then he sees a broken bottle and he realizes he won't live forever. Then some guy explains something and some people are going to be brought back to life, but nobody can find the cure. Then something won't work and a guy dies of cancer, and he's frozen, and something can't be repaired, then something else can't even be imagined, then some people get submerged in nitrogen and a guy bets his microscope and some worms don't give anybody a chance.

Those are all story events; they create a sense of forward movement. The movement is not toward a story ending, like, "And in that golden moment I realized that Nushka Resnikoff had saved me from the Chinese bandits and that I would make her my wife," but toward a complete body of information. The events are from the beginning of an article I wrote about Cryonics. It goes like this.

Do you know why a bottle of frozen milk breaks?

"Water expands when it freezes," says Dr. Roy Andersen, a professor of physics at Clark University. "Ice occupies more room than water, so the glass breaks."

You can probably get through life without this information, but the next time you see a broken bottle of frozen milk consider this: the fact that the bottle breaks is one reason why you probably won't live forever.

Andersen uses the analogy of the milk bottle to explain why he thinks cryonics won't work. "Cryonics," a word which has not earned its way into the dictionary, is the practice of freezing the newly dead, so that they can be brought back to life when a cure is found for whatever killed them.

As a legitimate science, its reputation among scientists ranks somewhere between phrenology and soothsaying. The reason?

"It simply won't work," Andersen says. "The body is mostly water. When you freeze a body the same thing that happens to the milk bottle takes place. The water expands and the cells are destroyed."

In other words, if a man died of cancer and was frozen, the discovery of a cancer cure would only begin to solve his problem. Scientists would also have to find a way to repair all those cells they destroyed when they froze him. And that, says Andersen, is a technology which can barely be imagined at this time. Virtually all of his colleagues would agree.

Nonetheless, there are at least five dead people in Berkeley, California, who would argue with Andersen if they could. They are at a place called Trans-Time Inc., comfortably submerged in liquid nitrogen, and they died fully confident that they would be returning someday. While Andersen would gladly bet his microscope that these people will stay dead, he would probably have to agree with Curtis Henderson, founder of the first cryonics society in the country, that their chances of coming back are "better than the worms and the crematoriums are going to give you."

So make sure that your nonfiction, as much as your fiction, has "something happening," and try to have at least one story event in each paragraph.

Transitions

A great way to put your reader into a coma is to use long transitions.

A transition is a phrase or sentence which takes the reader from one place, time, or subject, to the next. A transition should be short, direct, and almost invisible. In the manuscripts that I read I find that many writers are afraid of leaving something out, so they account for every moment and every movement. Patty meets Ted on Sunday night and she's smitten with him because he's a real cool guy. The next time she sees Ted is Tuesday. A good transition would be, "On Tuesday she saw Ted again." But the writer thinks the reader is going to notice that Monday is missing, so to explain Monday she writes a long transition like this:

> On Monday morning Patty was still daydreaming about Ted. When she got to work at nine o'clock she told her friend Trixie about how cool Ted was. At lunch time, with Ted still on her mind, she went to the same cafeteria where they had gone and she ate the same thing, a tuna fish on rye, with a side order of french fries smothered in turkey gravy. After lunch she thought about Ted while she sharpened her pencils, and on the bus home she saw a man who looked a little bit like Ted, but didn't have Ted's twinkling eyes, and it made her wonder if Ted ever took this same bus. She went to bed that night, still thinking of Ted, etc.

This sort of thing destroys the pace of your story. It is a sedative. You are not writing a calendar. If it's of no significance to the story, the reader doesn't care what happened on Monday.

Even writers who are comfortable writing, "She didn't see Ted until Tuesday night," are often uncomfortable with the simplicity of a transition that can cover three thousand miles or twenty years in a few words. They suspect that large amounts of time or space demand large amounts of words. Wrong. "Forty years later they met on the other side of the world," is a perfectly good transition. Or even, in a science fiction story, "Eighty million years later they met on a planet which didn't even exist when they were first introduced." There are no limits to the amount of time and space that can be covered by a simple transition. You should jump over everything that's not important, no matter how long it took or how much space it occupied.

Write this on a piece of paper and hang it over your desk:

A STORY IS NOT EVERYTHING THAT HAPPENED. IT'S EVERY IMPORTANT THING THAT HAPPENED.

AN ARTICLE IS NOT EVERYTHING THAT'S TRUE. IT'S EVERY IMPORTANT THING THAT'S TRUE.

If you have written an entire book that is moving too slowly, chances are you have written dozens of unnecessary scenes that should be replaced by simple transitions.

I received such a book from Ruth Rosing, a California writer who sent me a biography-in-progress of her late husband, Val Rosing. Val was an interesting guy, a womanizer, a gambler, the roller skating champion of Russia, and one of the most acclaimed opera singers and producers of his time. Ruth had done a fine job with her book, but she knew the pace was too slow.

I read it for her and I found that the story would speed along for ten or so pages and then hit a wall. That was because, like many writers, Ruth was writing scenes when she should have been writing transitions.

Val Rosing traveled often, and Ruth had the habit of taking the reader to the train station, putting him on the train with Val, showing him the scenery through the window, and so forth, when she should have gotten Val from place to place with a simple transition.

"Dear Ruth," I wrote. "You have a tendency to write entire scenes when all you need is a transition. If Val goes from Switzerland to Russia you should write, 'Val went to Russia' and then get on with what happened in Russia, unless something happened along the way that is important to your story, or reveals character. If the trip from Switzerland to Russia was uneventful, then don't include it. When you use several paragraphs to make a transition that could be made in a single sentence you are driving with your foot on the brake."

Ruth replaced all those unnecessary scenes with transitions and the book now has a much faster pace. Look at your manuscripts. Do you have unnecessary scenes? Do you have long passages where nothing eventful happens? Get rid of them. Here's another sign for you to hang over your desk:

WHEN YOU WRITE A STORY LEAVE OUT THE BORING STUFF.

Gasoline

A woman recently sent me a novel in which she had three paragraphs of details about a character cutting his finger and then bandaging it. I told the author that if the character eventually developed gangrene and died because of the cut, then perhaps those paragraphs would have been in proper proportion to the significance of the information they contained. She would have covered some ground with the fuel she had burned. But since the cut was a minor point, she had spent far too many words. She hadn't gotten good mileage.

Think of your words as gasoline and don't waste it. If you use two hundred words to tell the reader something important, fine. If you use two hundred words to say, "It was a beautiful morning" or "Dan waited in the street" or "Val went to Russia," you are getting lousy mileage.

Unity

Horace Walpole, whoever he is, said, "This world is a comedy to those who think, a tragedy to those who feel."

That's a nice quote. Unfortunately, it has nothing to do with unity in writing, so it shouldn't be in this chapter except to make this point: To achieve unity in your writing you must leave out anything that doesn't belong there, no matter how witty, poetic, or profound it is.

Unity, that quality of oneness in your writing, means that everything you write should look as if it were written at one time, by one person, with one purpose, using one language.

Why Is This So Important?

It's important because life is a mess. Well, maybe not a mess exactly, but life is just a bunch of stuff. It's random. You could slip on the ice and break your leg, or you could land safely and find a hundred dollar bill. Life isn't thinking, "This is a story about a guy who has good luck" or "This is a story about a guy who has bad luck." Life just sort of happens and we look at events later to figure out if they mean anything.

The fact that life just sprawls all over the place is kind of scary, and so human beings look to artists like you and me to organize life, to make sense out of it. Artists don't just paint a bunch of stuff; they paint pictures of things. Even the painter of abstracts seeks a unity which is called composition. Composers don't sit down at the piano and say, "Gee, I think I'll write a bunch of notes." They choose notes carefully to create an overall effect. In fact, to my mind, unity is as good a criterion as any for determining what is art and what is not.

Where there is no unity there is no sense of satisfaction. As a writer, you must aim for unity in everything that you write or you will not satisfy your readers. Don't just write a bunch of words. Write words that have something to do with each other.

Why Are You Telling Me This?

If I were to begin writing about wire now I would destroy the unity of this chapter. You would be disturbed by the question, "Why is he talking about wire?" But if I say that unity in your writing is made up of several smaller unities (unities of slant, tone, viewpoint, etc.), just as a length of wire is made up of several thinner strands of wire all going in the same direction, you will see immediately that wire has something to do with the subject at hand. You will not be disturbed because you will understand what wire has to do with unity in writing. You will know why I am talking about wire.

For every sentence that you write there should be an answer to the reader's implicit question, "Why is the writer telling me this?" Sometimes the answer can come later, but ninety-nine percent of the time, the answer should be obvious as soon as the reader reads the sentence.

The Reader Assumes Unity

In 1980 I spent three days in West Dennis, Massachusetts on Cape Cod. When I got home I found in my mail several sets of writer's guidelines from a publisher of romance novels. The publisher wanted me to hand them out to my writing students, which I did. But I kept one set and I said to myself, "Heh, heh, I could write one of these things."

At this time I owned a 1969, mustard-colored Ford Mustang, which had a broken headlight. So I studied the writer's guidelines and I wrote a book proposal of two chapters and an outline and I sent it to the publisher. About a month later an editor telephoned me and offered me a contract to write the novel.

Is anything bothering you? The Mustang perhaps, with the broken headlight? Of course it is. Because it doesn't seem to have anything to do with my story. When you read it you assumed it was part of the unity of my story. It didn't occur to you that the Mustang business popped out of the typewriter when I wasn't looking, or that I just put it in there for the hell of it. You figured it had something to do with everything else. And you politely waited to find out what. But after a few sentences went by, and I didn't mention the Mustang again, a voice in your mind began to nag you with the question, "What's the Mustang got to do with this?" If I had continued longer you might have forgotten about the specifics but you would know there was "something" that didn't make sense. You would be disturbed. The writing would be unsatisfying.

So that's my story. Now let's talk about Mona Erickson's story, and how she violated unity.

Mona, who lives in Cleveland, Ohio, sent me a story about a seventeen-year-old girl from Cleveland who takes a summer job at the New York World's Fair in 1964, meets a boy, and falls for him. It's a pleasant story about young love. But there is one scene in it where the girl's aunt, who lives in New York, comes to the girl's apartment and gives her a new typewriter, because the girl will be going off to college in the fall. There's a lot of material about how attractive the typewriter is and as I read the manuscript I just assumed that the typewriter scene had something to do with the story. Maybe the girl would write love letters on the typewriter. Maybe she would write a story about her New York experience. Maybe she would give the typewriter to her new boyfriend because he needs to write a ransom note. Something. But by the time the story ended and the sweethearts parted, the typewriter had not served any story purpose. It just sat there in the girl's room.

When I asked Mona why the typewriter was in the story she said, "Oh, no reason. But when I was in New York in 1964 that really happened. I've always remembered that day, and I thought it was such a touching, lovely thing for my aunt to do that I wanted to put that scene in for her."

Hmmn. Well, I'm sure Mona's aunt was a lovely lady, and I'm sure your aunt is equally wonderful, but don't put anything in to please her if it's not part of your story. The fact that something happens to be true is not a good reason to write about it. The fact that it's relevant is.

Unity of Slant

In writing nonfiction, you've learned that you can never write everything about a subject, so instead you write some things about a subject. What unifies those things is the slant. You can't write an article about volunteers. That's too broad. So you write an article about the shortage of volunteers for charitable organizations. To be part of your unity, every sentence you write must have something to do with the shortage of volunteers in charitable organizations.

It is easy to drift away from your unity. If you've learned interesting things in your research you tend to share them, even if they are irrelevant. But those paragraphs which violate the unity of your article will disturb your reader, so you must go back and remove them.

Let's say you've written the article about the shortage of volunteers in charitable organizations.

You wrote about the fact that traditionally the volunteers have been women and, with more women working outside the home, the pool of potential volunteers has become shallow.

You wrote about the fact that many charities have had to hire paid staff, and that has reduced the amount of money they can distribute to the needy.

You wrote about the fact that the new tax law will have an adverse effect on charities because only people who are itemizing can deduct for charitable contributions.

You wrote about the fact that charitable groups have become more aggressive in recruiting volunteers through phone calls and house calls.

Reread your article. With each paragraph don't ask only, "Is it a good paragraph?" And don't ask, "Is it a good paragraph about my subject?" Ask, "Is it a good paragraph relating to my particular slant on my subject?" You'll see that you wrote a paragraph or two about the new tax law. That material belongs in an article about tax deductions or charity fundraising, but not in one about the shortage of volunteers in charitable organizations. It violates the unity of your slant. Take it out.

Unity of Theme

For me "theme" was always one of those intimidating literary terms that made me afraid to be a writer. When I was twenty years old and had begun to write short stories, I lay awake nights, stricken with the fear that some creative writing teacher would say, "Gary, would you tell the class what the theme of your story is?" And, I, suddenly realizing that I had nothing original to say, would mumble some moronic cliché like "Virtue is its own reward." The class, of course, would howl with laughter, and I would spend part of the next day lugging my Remington typewriter to the Salvation Army. This never happened, but the reason I was tortured by such visions was that my high school English teachers, and probably yours, had made theme sound like some really big deal, and they had told me that my theme had to deliver some sort of message or moral.

Forget all that foolishness. There's no counting the number of writers who have been ruined by high school English teachers. Your theme is not a message or a moral. The theme of your story is whatever you answer when somebody says, "Hey, Marian, what's your story about?" That is not an unreasonable question. After all, if you saw a newspaper notice that said, "There will be a discussion at Hudson town hall tonight at 8 P.M." you would be perplexed. But if the notice also said "The theme of tonight's discussion is 'Should beach balls be outlawed in Hudson?' " you would have enough information to decide whether or not you wanted to go to the discussion. So if all you can say about your story is, "It's about a town that outlawed beach balls," that's enough. Keep in mind, however, that not all themes are good themes. A bad theme is one that imposes no limits on the writer. "Growing old," for example, is so vague that it is worthless. A good theme has walls around it; it has limits. "Growing old is better than the alternative," "A man grows old in a single moment," or "Three old men plan a bank robbery" would all be good themes.

You must know the theme of your story so that you will know when you have violated its unity.

Unity applies to theme in fiction in the same way that it applies to slant in nonfiction. Theme, like slant, is a junk detector. It tells you what to leave in and what to leave out. Leave in the stuff that relates to your theme. Take out everything else.

My wife Gail and I wrote a short story called "Streams" which, in another form, is chapter four in our book, *Good If It Goes*. If someone were to ask me what "Streams" is about, I would say, "It's about a boy named David who would rather play basketball than go to Hebrew school, and is trying to enlist his grandfather's help in the disagreement with the boy's parents."

Having said that, I now know the theme of the story and can look at every scene in the story and ask myself, "Does this relate to a boy who would rather play basketball, etc.?"

In scene one the family goes to Newton, where the grandfather lives. (Yes, this relates to our theme because David is going to see his grandfather and he's thinking about his persuasion strategy.)

In scene two the family goes to temple. (Yes, because the whole weight of the parents' argument is that David must keep his Jewish tradition. If the family had gone to a truck pull we would have a hard time defending that as part of our unity.)

In scene three the boy and his grandfather walk down to a stream where the boy brings up the problem. (Yes. This is the heart of the story.)

In scene four the boy and his grandfather walk back to the house where they celebrate Rosh Hashanah. (Is this part of the unity of the theme? Yes, because the grandfather has taken the parents' side, but he has also taught David the importance of tradition. If they had come back and celebrated a birthday, or someone's promotion at the umbrella factory, we would have violated our unity, and we would take the scene out.)

Unity of Style

Style is not what you write, but how you write it. You can write your story or article any way you want, but to preserve the unity and hold your reader you should write all of it the same way.

Your writing style is the personality that you bring to a piece of writing. Some writers bring the same personality to every piece. Others change personality, depending on the material. Neither is right or wrong. What's wrong is changing personalities in the middle of a piece. Here is some material which I wrote in my journal in 1974 when I was living in Florida, and had been operating a switchboard at a Miami Beach hotel. Some names have been changed to protect the weird.

> I quit my job last week. No big deal, just got tired of it. Anyhow it gives Miss Daley a chance to hire yet another relative. And it is Miss Daley, you understand. In the year and a half that I have known her she has never allowed anybody to say "Claudia" to her even though that's her name. Nothing wrong with that woman's head, right? I mean the president is Dick to the people in his office, cardinals call the pope Paul, and even God doesn't expect the an-

gels to call him Mr. God, but here is this borderline illiterate woman who is convinced that she is a Miss Daley and not a Claudia. This Daley family is a bit bizarre . . . mentally suspect, genetically unsound . . . most of them conceived through an unlaundered sock. Anyhow, Miss Daley's mother died last week, just croaked on the third day, leaving a note that said, you've been a good daughter, Miss Daley, don't grieve for me. So here comes Miss Daley's granddaughter, one of three misshappen, unread, skull-faced daughters of Miss Daley's florid-faced, beer-drinking, glassy-eyed, 53 year old sales clerk of a daughter, comes flying in from Frisco where she lives with her airman third class 18 year old husband and their undoubtedly strange looking baby whatsit that's three months older than their shaky marriage. . . .

As you can see, the style I used there was quite different from, say, the style of this book or one of my novels. But, though the style is different, it has unity. It sounds as if it is being spoken in a single voice. One feature of that style is a lot of long sentences. If I suddenly stopped using long sentences I would violate the unity of style. Of course a variety of sentence lengths is important in all of your writing, and we'll discuss that in depth later, but the important thing here is that even the variety must be consistent. If you use mostly long sentences for several paragraphs, you create an expectation by the reader that a lot of long sentences are part of the unity of the piece. You will destroy that if you suddenly shift to all short and medium-length sentences.

Other features of that excerpt are a reckless disregard for the rules of punctuation, and invented words like "whatsit" and a lot of hyphenated phrases. In the example below you will hear what happens when I violate the unity of my style by abandoning my long sentences and suddenly adopting orthodox punctuation.

Anyhow, Miss Daley's mother died last week, just croaked on the third day, leaving a note that said, you've been a good daughter, Miss Daley, don't grieve for me. So here comes Miss Daley's granddaughter, one of three misshapen, unread, skull-faced daughters of Miss Daley's florid-faced, beer-drinking, glassy-eyed, 53 year old sales clerk of a daughter, comes flying in from Frisco where she lives with her airman-third-class 18 year old husband and their undoubtedly strange looking baby whatsit that's three months older than their shaky marriage. The girl's name is

Marie. She's a short red-head with a face covered with freckles. Her husband, Lucas, works at a gas station. That's where he accidentally lost his thumb while checking someone's car for oil. Apparently he didn't know the difference between a fan and a dipstick.

In that example the material is the same, but the style used to convey it changes suddenly in the last five sentences. The unity of style is violated and the reading process is disrupted.

To avoid violating the unity of your style in a story or article, read the first four paragraphs of an early draft and ask yourself, what are the characteristics of the style? Are there a lot of long sentences? Are there a lot of very short sentences? Does the writer seem to be a comma conservative or a comma liberal? Is there one thought in most sentences, or do most of the sentences contain clauses and flash multiple images before the reader? Do the paragraphs contain several words that would only be known to a particular type of reader?

Now look at the last four paragraphs and ask yourself the same questions. You should come up with the same answers. If not, it could be that you have changed style somewhere along the way. Read the piece over and listen for the change. If you listen carefully and you still can't hear it, then it's probably not significant enough for you to worry about.

A change of style is most likely to occur when you have begun a story, then left it alone for several weeks and returned to it in a different frame of mind. In the next section we'll see how a vacation from a manuscript violated the unity of tone, but the point could just as well apply to style.

Unity of Tone

Because tone and style influence each other so much, it would be easy to confuse them. For that reason I limited my examples of style in the last section to things that you could *see* . . . long sentences, punctuation, etc. Tone is more of an attitude, a message that you send the reader about how the material should be experienced. Your tone can be humorous, serious, nostalgic, cynical, whatever. There's no right tone. You choose it. But once you choose it, stick with it. Don't violate the unity of the tone by shifting suddenly from idealistic to cynical, or from serious to humorous.

For example:

In recent years I've learned something that I wish I had known when I was a teenager, longing for a girlfriend. I've learned that every woman, as much as every man, is insecure. We're all made out of the same stuff. We're all part adult ready to deal with people, and part child crouching in the attic whenever company comes.

I grew up believing that females were the attractive ones, the desirable ones, the valuable ones. Certainly they were more valuable than I felt.

How was I to know that back then they would have enthusiastically dated any pimply-faced, hawk-nosed, club-footed pariah who cranked up enough gumption to call them? How was I to know that while I was home popping corn on Saturday night these girls were out with guys just like me, freckle-faced midgets with knots of Brylcreem in their hair and cheeks that reeked of Hawaiian Surf?

This piece begins with a serious tone. The writer, it seems, has something meaningful to say about insecurity and how helpful it would be if each of us understood that members of the opposite sex were as insecure as we are. But in the third paragraph, the serious tone gives way to one of comedy. The writer is no longer taking the subject seriously. He's having fun with it. At that point the unity of tone has been broken. Either tone is fine. But they cannot coexist in the same piece.

For a fiction example, let us learn from the mistake of Claire Volk. Claire, a writer from Nashville, Tennessee, sent me a story. She told me that an editor who rejected it told her the tone was uneven. Claire wanted me to explain what he meant.

The story was based on a real incident in her life. She had been assaulted by a handyman, who apparently intended to rape her but was scared off by her screams.

The early passages of the story are filled with the fear, the indignation, the sense of vulnerability being felt by the character based on Claire.

She could feel the wall pressing against her back. There was nowhere to go. As he moved toward her she tried to scream but nothing came out.

So the tone is set. The writer is saying to the reader, this is a deadly serious situation. And yet when we get to the end of the story we read:

I learned later that Fred had tried this with other women. I guess he had his work day set up just the way he wanted it: a little work, a little sex, a little work, a little sex.

That humorous ending violates the tone. It jars the reader. The reader feels confused. "You told me to feel this way, now you're telling me to feel completely different," he thinks.

When I explained this to Claire she told me that she had written most of the story shortly after the real incident, and the ending much later. That's what I had guessed. It's not uncommon for us to joke about serious, even frightening, matters when they are safely behind us. It's probably even healthy. But Claire's readers didn't have that six months. They got the serious tone followed immediately by the humorous tone, and they were in no mood to joke about what had just happened.

Unity of Viewpoint

I've written a chapter on viewpoint so I won't belabor the subject here. Briefly, unity of viewpoint doesn't mean that you can use only one viewpoint in a story. It means that your use of viewpoint should appear to have some overall pattern. If you wrote a book in which odd-numbered chapters were written in the omniscient viewpoint, and even-numbered chapters were in character viewpoint, the reader would get a sense of unity. But if you wrote fifteen chapters in the omniscient viewpoint and then switched to character viewpoint for the last two chapters, the reader would be disturbed by the questions, "How come the writer is doing this differently now? Is this the same book, or what?"

In viewpoint, as in other aspects of your writing, several changes can create a unity of their own, but a single change will be unsettling.

Unity of Premise

If an article has a slant, and a short story has a theme, what does a column have? It has a premise, a basic statement that the author wants to communicate. The premise gives the column unity. When the premise is abandoned the unity is broken and the reader is lost.

Sometimes the premise is stated right at the beginning of the column, as when Andy Rooney says something like, "Did you ever wonder how vegetables got their names?" Just as often the premise is implicit.

Most of the writers who sent me column manuscripts to critique made the mistake of forgetting the premise. Typically, the writer began a column with a definite idea in mind, but her mind wandered. She thought of something clever or profound to say, and she wrote it in, even if it had nothing to do with the premise of her column.

This mistake is particularly rampant among writers of humor columns. They can't pass up a good joke even when it destroys the unity of their column.

One of the funniest people to send me pages was Lou Burnett, from Warner Robins, Georgia. Lou is a humorist, and he was regularly getting his columns published in a few smaller-town newspapers. But he wanted advice that would help him improve his columns so that he could take a shot at bigger markets and maybe syndication. Lou wrote in a nice personable style. He created the same voice in every column, which is essential for a regular column. He was consistent in the length of his pieces, the style, and the format of short paragraphs. All of this was important, because the reader of a regular column looks for the familiar. She wants this week's column to look a lot like last week's column.

The major weakness in Lou's columns was his inability to remain focused all the way to the end, to maintain that unity of premise.

"Dear Lou," I wrote. "You're a very funny guy, but a lot of people can write ten funny things. The trick is to write ten funny things on one subject. The reader will lose interest if he feels that you are reaching. Who's more interesting, the guy who tells three funny jokes, or the guy who can tell three funny jokes on any subject you name?"

Lou had sent three columns to me. The first was called "The Gooney Birds," and the implicit premise of the column was "everything here relates to the DC-3 and I'm writing about that plane now because this is its 50th anniversary."

The first paragraphs were fine. They all related to the airplane. But when Burnett finished an anecdote about parachuting out of the airplane, he wrote another anecdote about parachuting, which could have applied to any airplane. The anecdote sounded like something that Lou just happened to remember while writing, and it seemed unrelated to the DC-3. The unity of the premise had been broken, the focus lost, and the reader left without bearings.

The second column was called "Weather or Not," and the premise of it was, "What if government committees chose the weather?" Like the first, it was quite funny, but again when Lou ran out of material to support his premise, he started reaching. Toward the end of the column he began writing about "What if we were granted supreme power for weather?" but everything before that had been based on the joke of government committees trying to choose weather. His tightly focused joke was "government committees" and now he had switched to "people in general."

My advice to Lou, and my advice to you, is to have a strong sense of limits for each column. What exactly is your column about? Write it down on a piece of paper. After you've drafted your column go back through the manuscript. Look at each paragraph. Ask, is it funny, strong, pointed? Then ask, "Does it fit with the premise that I have written on the piece of paper?" Don't cling to any material just because it's funny or sounds clever. Be sure that it belongs in that particular column. You'll have to take out many lines that you are fond of. That's okay. You don't have to cremate them. File them and use them in a column where they do belong.

By the way, violating the unity of your premise is not the same as expanding the premise. Expanding the premise is perfectly okay, as long as you don't do it halfway through your column. Let's say you're writing a column about funny things that happen to teenaged boys. Then in paragraph three you break your premise by writing about a funny thing that happens to teenaged girls. And then you think of another funny thing that happens to teenaged girls, and then another. Instead of taking out all the girl material you can expand your premise to "funny things that happen to teenagers." But when you rewrite, make that your premise from the beginning.

Unity of premise also applies to the longer essays, such as the "Chronicle" section of *Writer's Digest* or the "My Turn" section in *Newsweek*. These pieces often cover broader ground, but they still require unity.

In one "My Turn" essay, "Trials of an Expert Witness," Elizabeth Loftus, a Jewish psychologist who specializes in memory, writes about being asked to help in the defense of John Demjanjuk, a man accused of killing millions of Jews in Poland during World War II.

Early in the piece she writes:

"Given my own Jewish heritage and strong feelings about the crime, could I possibly testify on Demjanjuk's behalf?

"I spent two months thinking about it. What of the presumption of innocence? And what of my own obligations to my science and of my science to the community at large?"

Here she has set down the premise: people are uncomfortable when they find inconsistency in themselves.

If Loftus had drifted into a discussion of inconsistency in public policy, or started writing other things that make people uncomfortable, she would have violated her premise.

In the end, she chose not to defend the man accused of the war crimes. She writes:

"Not to act consistently feels intellectually dishonest. But what about Uncle Joe and Jeremy's mother and the five survivors who would feel so terribly betrayed? It's as if I were being asked to testify for the man accused of killing my brother. My friend, quoting Emerson, reminded me that, 'A foolish consistency is the hobgoblin of little minds.'

"Emerson was comforting. I decided to leave this case to my colleagues. The cost of testifying as a defense witness would have been too great for the people I love most."

Here she is telling us how she dealt with the inconsistency, but she has not changed the premise. At the end she is saying the same thing she said at the beginning: inconsistency is uncomfortable.

Unity of Material

When Marie Melville of Wilmington, North Carolina, became a widow she learned that she was not equipped to deal with banking, car repairs, dating, and a variety of other issues which either never arose during her married life, or had been taken care of by her husband. As she learned to cope with these matters she kept notes, so that she could communicate her new knowledge to readers in the same situation. She wrote a book about how to adjust to widowhood and she sent the manuscript to me for evaluation.

This was a good book idea. There was an identifiable audience for the book, and Marie had accumulated a lot of good service information—that is, information that the reader could use.

The reason that the book was not publishable when I got it was that Marie, understandably inspired to write it by her own tragedy, included a great deal of autobiographical material concerning her husband and her own widowhood. A small amount of this material would have been okay, even valuable, because it would give the book a personal tone. But approximately half the book was Marie's personal story material, which had no service value to the reader. It violated the unity which said, "This is a nuts and bolts service book of material which is useful to the reader."

I told Marie to write her own experience only in those places where her problem could be used to demonstrate a solution to the reader's problem. I told her to take out all the rest of her personal material and try to harness its power for another book, perhaps a novel.

For a book to get published and sell well it has got to be either fish or fowl, not a fish with wings or a bird with fins. There are successful exceptions to this rule, but they are rare.

In writing the proposal for this book, if I had included a few chapters on how to sell what you write, the publishers would have said, "Well, what exactly is it, Gary, a marketing book or a technique book?" I would have to decide between the two. (That's if I were given the opportunity. Usually if an author seems unclear as to what exactly his book is, the publisher will simply reject it.) Certs can be a breath mint and a candy mint at the same time, but most books cannot.

A few years ago I wrote a proposal for a book called *You Can Play*. It was a book for all the people who felt as if they were picked last for baseball when they were kids (which is just about everybody, even though that would require a dramatic new theory of arithmetic). Each of the twenty-two chapters in my book would cover a participant sport. In each chapter I would 1) Give the reader a short history of the sport; 2) Assure her that she could play the sport even if she was an overweight, undernourished, insecure klutz, and 3) Provide her with the nuts and bolts information about how to get involved with the sport, what to wear, etc. I thought of *You Can Play* as a self-help, how-to, sports book.

I sent it to an editor at William Morrow and Co. He telephoned me the day he got it. He loved it. I thought for sure I had a book sale. But when it went to committee for approval, which is what most books have to do these days, it got shot down.

The editor called me up.

"They liked it but they don't want to publish it," he said.

"Why?"

"Because they don't know what it is."

"Excuse me," I said, "I seem to be having some trouble with my phone. What was that, again?"

"They don't know where we would put it in the book store," he explained. "Does it go in the self-help section, the how-to section, or the sports section?"

Now, I have never agreed with any publisher's reason for rejecting a book of mine, but this one was particularly repugnant. Why not just put the book in all three sections and maybe sell three times as many books?

I sent the book proposal to a few other publishers and heard somewhat the same feeble excuse for not publishing it. In effect, they were saying that the book didn't have unity of material.

So if you have a book or an idea for a book that you want to publish, ask yourself what shelf it would go on in the book store. If you come up with more than one answer, choose a shelf, then go back into the manuscript and cut out most of the material that would land it on the other shelf. Who knows? You might come up with two books.

Creating Unity in a Book

Have you noticed that every chapter in this book is printed in the same typeface on the same kind of paper? Weird coincidence, huh? Of course not. It's just that readers are so demanding of unity that we give most of it to them without even thinking about it. We don't even consider the alternatives. Intuitively we know that the reader demands unity. We never start a story in the first person and end it in the third person.

There are dozens of these unities and most of them are easy to decide on.

But when you begin a book there is one decision that is never easy. What's going to hold the book together? What is it that will create the illusion that everything you write belongs in the book and everything you don't write doesn't belong in the book? What thread will run through the book and give the reader a sense of its unity?

When you write a novel, the choice of unity is usually not separated from the decision to write the novel. There are organizational problems, but generally speaking, the unity *is* the novel. The plot is what holds it together. Usually you have a story with a beginning, a middle, and an end. You move from birth to death, from first date to wedding, from job interview to "take this job and shove it." You usually move in a straight line through time from the first day to the last day. If you had no sense of unity you probably wouldn't consider the material as a novel in the first place.

But in nonfiction this is not usually the case. You have two decisions to make: What material am I going to use and how am I going to unify that material?

Your nonfiction material, whether you are writing a book or an article, usually comes to you as a bunch of information. The information doesn't know that you are writing a book, so it doesn't take the trouble to arrive in any organized fashion. When you interview one expert on horse racing you learn everything he can tell you. Then you interview another expert on horse racing and you learn everything she can tell you. But since you are writing a book about horse racing, not a book about experts, you can't write the information in the order that you got it.

When I wrote *Fatal Dosage,* the true story of a nurse on trial for murder, I didn't have this problem. A patient had died. A nurse had been accused of deliberately overdosing the patient with morphine. There was an investigation. The nurse was fired. The newspapers got the story. There was a grand jury inquiry. There were indictments. There was a trial. And so on. The unity was obvious: just tell the story the way it happened, Gary. So I began with the day the nurse found out about the patient, and ended with the verdict.

But when I began to write *Finder,* the story of Marilyn Greene, a real woman who finds missing people, I had a problem.

I knew I had exciting material that would make for a successful book, but I didn't know what the unity would be. I didn't know how to tie it all together. I knew the book had to be primarily about Marilyn's investigative career, but her career was still in progress.

I could have divided *Finder* up into case histories, with each chapter being a new case, but then the book would have been episodic. A book is episodic when it seems to be a series of events or incidents that are isolated from each other, rather than combining to create a sense of forward movement. "It's too episodic," is one of the more common explanations for why a publisher is rejecting a book.

So I couldn't write the book as a series of case histories. Nobody would buy it. Instead, I did what all writers do. I stared at the material and gnashed my teeth.

Then I got lucky.

Marilyn's seventeen-year-old son, Paul, ran away from home.

While this was bad news for Marilyn, it was good news for me. The son of the finder of missing persons was now a missing person. I could use the period of his absence as a kind of bracket to hold the book together.

Here's how I used Paul's disappearance to unify the book.

Finder is written in the first person, as if Marilyn were telling the story. To get the reader immediately involved I opened with a case in progress, the Rachel Achorn case, proceeded to the start of a few other cases and then wrote:

> Local police departments have their own computers which can call up information from the NCIC. If, for example, Peter were picked up for vagrancy in Miami, the Miami police would run his name through the NCIC and find the information that the police had put in there. They would call the local police. The local police would call Peter's parents and the parents would take it from there.

> After I did that I started work on a few other cases. But something happened that brought everything to a halt. My own son disappeared.

Of course, as I began the book Marilyn's son was still missing. If he wasn't found by the time I finished the manuscript I would be in big trouble. But I guessed that he would show up, and so, ten paragraphs later, I used his disappearance as the door that would lead us into the body of the book: Marilyn's eighteen-year career.

> By one o'clock in the morning I was afraid that Paul was dead. That fear is not quite as hysterical as it might seem. Three people had been murdered in Albany county in the past six weeks. All of them had been hitchhiking.

> By two o'clock I was certain that Paul was okay, that he would come home to me a better person, that we would find out once and for all what was going on inside of him and we would straighten it out. But I couldn't get it out of my mind that I was somehow responsible. Could Paul's anguish be traced to my own career? Had I spent too much time looking for other people's kids and not enough looking after my own?

For the next 250 pages I covered Marilyn's career in somewhat chronological fashion. But the strand that held it together was the growth in her personal life, specifically scenes which showed Paul becoming the troubled child who would eventually run away.

In the last part of the book Paul is found and the last scene in the book is of Marilyn and Paul having lunch in Vermont where they have both been searching for a missing child.

> After lunch Paul walked me to the front door of the motel. I told

him I'd come back to get him in a couple of days and wished him
luck with the search.

"When I get home can I have a dog?" he said.

"Paul, we already have two dogs."

"I know. But I want one that's mine. You know, to train, so I can
help you in searches."

"You want to go on searches?" I said. I could feel a tightness in my
throat and my eyes were suddenly wet with tears. Perhaps I would
never find Rachel Achorn, I thought, but I had found my son.

There were a few more paragraphs before the book ended, but I
had shown the reader the other end of the unity strand that began with
"my own son had disappeared." This was not a book about Marilyn's
son disappearing. It was a book about her career, but his disappearance
was the thing that held it all together.

Here's another example. I talked to Joe McGinniss, author of *Fatal Vision*, about this. Joe had written a book called *Going to Extremes*,
about Alaska and the people who go there with their dreams. He told me
that after he's taken his notes, and before he goes to the typewriter for
the first draft, he has to go through the decision-making process about
the unity of the book, which is, he said, "the hardest part of every
book."

"The organizational problems are awful," he said. "What do you
put in, what do you leave out? In the Alaska book, putting the ferry ride
in was obvious, but then what? I used to get up in the morning and say,
'What should I do today? Should I go to Fairbanks? Should I go to Ko-
diak?' It can paralyze you. In the end I found a pattern for the book. I developed it from cold to warmth, from darkness to light, from those
whose lives were screwed up by Alaska to those who were fulfilled. But
to do that you sometimes have to rearrange things. For example, the
Brooks Range section comes at the end of the book, but it really came at
the end of my first summer there. And in between there are so many
false trails. Sometimes I'd put in weeks, even months, gathering material, and then deciding I can't use it. It might be interesting but it's not part
of what I'm doing."

"It's not part of what I'm doing," is another way of saying it would
violate the unity of the book.

Here are some of the common ways that writers give book material
a sense of unity.

1. Alphabetically. If you're writing a book of celebrity profiles, a consumer report on new cars, or "The Language of Beer Brewing," you could arrange your topics alphabetically and the reader would have a sense of unity. He would know why Zymurgy, the science and study of fermentation in brewing, was at the back of the book.

2. Chronologically. If you are writing the history of computers, or an analysis of the Reagan presidency, you could start with the first event and finish with the last. The reader would have the sense of unity.

3. East to west, north to south, etc. If you were writing "The Twenty Most Interesting Cities of the World" or "Weather Patterns of the Western Hemisphere" you could move always in one direction.

What about you? How would you arrange these books?

1. *Being There: The top 100 annual events in America.*
2. *Glitter and Green: The inside story of Hollywood today.*
3. *I Say to You This: Advice about life and stuff from Major Garonovitch.*
4. *Weather Is My Life: The Autobiography of Randy Freidus.*
5. *Raising Buster: How to Train Your Dog.*

Now stop for a moment and think about the chapter you have just read. Did it sound to you as if it were all written during one visit to the typewriter? Do I sound now like the same Gary who was speaking to you at the beginning of the chapter? Do you feel that you understood the overall point of the chapter? Does it seem to you that I am working with the same vocabulary I started with, expressing myself in the same ways, delivering pretty much the same message about the material?

If the answer to all the questions is "Yes," then I have succeeded in creating unity for this chapter. I have practiced what I preached in the beginning when I told you that everything you write should look as if it were written at one time, by one person, with one purpose, using one language.

Sound

You are perhaps having some auditory difficulty in perceiving my attempts to achieve communication with you. Let me make a few adjustments here. Okay, can you hear me now? Is it clear? Sure it is. That's because I've created a sound you like, one you recognize and easily comprehend. It's the sound of conversation.

Writing Is a Symphony

Writing is not a visual art. It is a symphony, not an oil painting. It is the shattering, not the glass. It is the ringing, not the bell. The words you write make sounds, and when the sounds satisfy the reader's ear, your writing works. Note that I said "satisfy," not "please." We writers want satisfied readers, not necessarily happy readers. If your reader's heart starts to pound and his palms begin to sweat because you have placed in your horror story a word that startles him like a shriek from the attic, he is not happy, but he is satisfied.

I can't teach you everything you need to know about sound in writing. To a large extent you just have to develop a good ear for writing, and nobody can help you do that. If you're not feeling confident about this, consider the fact that you probably hear dozens of grammatical mistakes even though you don't know the grammatical rule that's being broken. That's because you have developed an ear for grammar. You know something's wrong because it sounds wrong. The same process applies to your writing. If you write every day you will develop that ear to the point where you know that "it just doesn't sound right." Eventually you will begin to understand *why* it doesn't sound right.

Write Short, Medium, and Long Sentences

Da da da da da da. Da da da da da da. Da da da da da da. Da da da da da da. Da da da da da da. (Getting bored yet?) Da da da da da da. Da da da da da da. Da da da da da da. (How about now?) Da da da da da da. Da da da da da da.

By now you're probably getting disgusted, so I'd better move forward. The monotonous sound that you hear in the first paragraph is the sound you will make in the reader's head if you write several sentences in a row that have approximately the same length. The ear must have variety or the mind will go out to lunch. You wouldn't listen to a singer who sang the same song over and over. You wouldn't watch a movie that played the same scene fifteen times. And you won't read something that makes the same noise sentence after sentence.

Listen to this example of what a series of short sentences can do.

> We're going to be ruthless about this. We're going to be direct. Renault still has its problems. Renault cars betray their origins. They display Gallic idiosyncrasies. Renault fans are still absent. Hordes of them are in the European markets. The life-blood of commerce is finance. But Renault has countless punctured arteries. They must be stitched up.

> The French taxpayer is its guardian angel. Overmanning problems have been reduced. They are 22 percent lower in the past two years. Things are slowly changing. Da da da da da da. Da da da da da da. Da da da da da da.

How long would you keep reading something like that? Not long, probably. It's boring because all of the sentences are short and they create a monotonous sound in the reader's ear.

Here's how Phillip Bingham actually wrote it in *Motor Trend* magazine.

> We're going to be ruthlessly direct about this. Renault still has its problems. Renault cars still betray their origins through Gallic idiosyncrasies. Renault fans are still absent in hordes in several of France's neighboring European markets. And, if the life-blood of commerce is finance, Renault still has countless punctured arteries to stitch up.
>
> But, with the French taxpayer as its guardian angel, and with its overmanning problems reduced by 22 percent in the past two years, things are slowly changing for the better at Renault. Including the cars.

Now, let's listen to a fiction example to see how several long sentences can cause the same problem.

> Waking, he saw aqueous light on the blue-white ceiling—the morning sun reflected from the swimming pool just outside the window, and the moment he raised his head the poison struck; thirst, nausea, a barbed pain behind the eyes. When he turned he felt the warm girl beside him, naked, belly down, and he reached out, and with the lightest touch his sodden state could bring to bear, ran his fingers along the small of her back, over her buttocks and firm thigh. In his first moments of consciousness, he had not been able to remember who it was there, but the touch of her cool young skin brought recollection quickly enough.
>
> As gently and silently as he could, he climbed out of bed and padded across the tiles to the chair on which he had piled his clothes the night before, not wanting to wake her, wanting to be alone in spite of his loneliness.
>
> Dressed, he went out through the bedroom and found himself in her enormous kitchen, which was stark white, gleaming with steel and glass, resplendent with morning, and at the tap he drank long and breathlessly, resting his elbows on the cold edge of the sink, where he wet his hand and rubbed his face. When he looked up he saw brown mountains through the kitchen window, a steep ridge crowned with mist commanding a neat green valley, and he could see that it was a shimmering day, dappled with promise. Da da da

da da da da da da, da da da da da da da, da da da da da da da da da da da da da da da, da da da da da da da da.

Long and breathlessly, indeed. Your reader will not stick around long enough to notice what kind of a day it is if you assault him with a series of long sentences like those. You must vary the length of your sentences so that they create a pleasing sound. Here is how Robert Stone really wrote that passage in *Children of Light* (Knopf).

Waking, he saw aqueous light on the blue-white ceiling—the morning sun reflected from the swimming pool just outside the window. The moment he raised his head the poison struck; thirst, nausea, a barbed pain behind the eyes. When he turned he felt the warm girl beside him, naked, belly down. He reached out, and with the lightest touch his sodden state could bring to bear, ran his fingers along the small of her back, over her buttocks and firm thigh. In his first moments of consciousness, he had not been able to remember who it was there. The touch of her cool young skin brought recollection quickly enough.

As gently and silently as he could, he climbed out of bed and padded across the tiles to the chair on which he had piled his clothes the night before. He did not want to wake her, wanted to be alone in spite of his loneliness.

Dressed, he went out through the bedroom door and found himself in her enormous kitchen. It was stark white, gleaming with steel and glass, resplendent with morning. At the tap, he drank long and breathlessly, resting his elbows on the cold edge of the sink. He wet his hands and rubbed his face. When he looked up he saw brown mountains through the kitchen window, a steep ridge crowned with mist commanding a neat green valley. It was a shimmering day, dappled with promise.

Here are some numbers for you: 25, 14, 12, 3, 21, 33, 28, 8, 12, 35, 51, 16, 33, 4.

Those are the numbers of words in the first fourteen sentences of Mark Twain's *The Adventures of Huckleberry Finn,* a book that sold well. I rest my case.

Vary the Construction of Your Sentences

Wolf raised the flag.

Ollie North and Gordon Liddy swapped pistols.

The big green billboard on Colorado Avenue swayed in the wind, then toppled over onto Sturge Thibedeau's new Cadillac convertible.

Those three sentences are of different lengths. But they are all constructed the same way. Each begins with the subject, moves directly to the predicate, and ends with the object. When we first learn to write, we are taught to put the elements of a sentence in that order. It is the most logical, most easily understood construction. Most of your sentences should be built this way.

However, just as there should be variety in the length of your sentences, there should be variety in their shape. You should change the sentence construction from time to time in a way that creates a pleasant music. The subjects, the predicates and the objects should all, from time to time, dance to surprising places.

If several sentences in a row are all constructed the same way they will create a drone that will bore readers. Here's an example.

> She slipped into a window seat in the nonsmoking section and placed a slim black case on her lap and leafed through its contents. She latched the case once the plane was in the air, then she glanced briefly at the sunlit Manhattan skyline, let her head fall back, and closed her eyes.
>
> Anne Ellis, thirty-two, was a senior editor at Castle Press, a highly successful publishing house on lower Park Avenue. She was flying to Washington to meet with a man named Hamilton Carver. Every sizable publishing house in New York had sought a meeting with Carver for years. Carver was a financier, developer, and womanizer who was surrounded by a battery of lawyers and a cadre of bodyguards and he had played as large a part as any man could in changing the face of the eastern seaboard of the United States in the years since 1960. Little was known of his personal life.

That's my rewrite of the first chapter of Douglass Wallop's novel, *The Other Side of the River* (W.W. Norton). I would have to go on quite a bit longer to make it really boring, but I think in those two paragraphs you can begin to hear the monotonous sound created when several sentences in a row are constructed the same way.

Now listen to the difference when variety in construction is added to the music. This is how Wallop wrote those first two paragraphs.

> Slipping into a window seat in the nonsmoking section, she placed a slim black case on her lap and leafed through its contents. Once the plane was in the air, she latched the case, glanced briefly at the sunlit Manhattan skyline, let her head fall back, and closed her eyes.

> At thirty-two, Anne Ellis was a senior editor at Castle Press, a highly successful publishing house on lower Park Avenue. She was flying to Washington for a meeting with a man named Hamilton Carver. A meeting with Carver had been sought for years by every sizable publishing house in New York. Financier, developer, womanizer, surrounded by a battery of lawyers and a cadre of bodyguards, Carver in the years since 1960 had played as large a part as any one man could in changing the face of the eastern seaboard of the United States. Little was known of his personal life.

Experiment with Parallel Construction

Though several sentences in a row with the same construction can bore the reader, there are times when you will deliberately build two or three consecutive sentences the same way to create a sound and an emphasis that serves your purpose. This is known as parallel construction. Here's an example.

> *Without parallel construction:*
> Worcester County is a wonderful place for a vacation any time of the year. Mt. Wachussett is available for skiing. Golf courses are easy to find. Several lakes in the area offer fishing opportunities. The foliage in Worcester county is among the most beautiful in the area.

> *With parallel construction:*
> Worcester County is a wonderful place for a vacation any time of the year. You can ski in Worcester County. You can golf in Worcester County. You can fish in Worcester County. You can view beautiful foliage in Worcester County.

The parallel construction in the last sentences makes the premise of the first sentence more convincing.

Writing Should Sound Like Speech

The effective writer satisfies his reader by creating sentences and paragraphs that sound like conversation. My first wordy sentence at the beginning of this chapter created an unsatisfactory sound, not because you didn't know the meaning of the words, but because the words were not primary words; that is, they were not words that reveal their meaning instantly. You needed time to stop and think, "auditory—what does that mean?" But I didn't give you time. I kept talking, adding more words that required a second for translation. And so my words became as meaningless as the static on a cheap radio. If I had continued that way, you would have stopped listening.

So good writing sounds like conversation because it uses the simple primary words of conversation, words that say what they mean and say it immediately. Good writing, like conversation, also uses the variety of sentence length that we've discussed. And good writing contains the frequent breaks or pauses of conversation. When we talk we rarely use a sentence of more than twenty-five words. We say, "I went to Watertown yesterday. Ran into Ron and Marcia. Marcia looks great. Ron's got this job working for some kind of school for the blind right there in Watertown. I'm not sure what he does. Publicity, I think. I'll tell you one thing, though, I'm never going to drive through Watertown on a Saturday again, not with all that traffic. Horrendous!"

Good writing *sounds* like conversation. It doesn't duplicate it. The person in conversation is always working in the first draft and he has no word limit; he does not choose his words with great care and he does not economize the way a writer must. The speaker says, "I saw this fox . . . It was brown and had a long tail. Anyhow, it came over to where Buddy, that's Jim's dog, was sleeping. You remember Buddy. Jim's dog, the one that's always sleeping on the back porch of his cottage up in— what's the name of that town? Winchendon—that's it. Anyhow, this fox came up to where Buddy was lying and just sort of jumped over him real fast and then he went dashing off into the woods. There's some beautiful woods up there. I found out later that the fox does this all the time."

The writer has to make every word count, so he writes, "The quick brown fox jumps over the lazy dog."

Also remember that being conversational in your writing does not mean being chatty. Here is an example of a writer trying to be chatty, not conversational:

> Want to learn more about being an equine practitioner? Hey, no problem! Get to know some. They'll talk. They'll share. They'll fill you in on what it's all about. They'll give you valuable tips. After all, they've been around. They've seen it all. They know what can happen.

That, of course, is not the way my friend Ron Trahan wrote it in his book, *Careers for Horse Lovers* (Houghton Mifflin). He wrote:

> One of the best ways to learn more about the career of an equine practitioner is to become acquainted with one. Most are usually willing and eager to discuss their careers. Their information can be invaluable. After all, they've successfully combated and surmounted all of the problems typically encountered.

Use Complete Sentences Often. Fragments Rarely.

Ninety-nine percent of the time you should use complete sentences in your writing. The reader expects a subject and a predicate to greet him every time he begins to read a sentence. He listens for them. If he doesn't hear them he is disturbed. Something just doesn't sound right. Awkward. Like here. And here. Sentence fragments. See? Not good.

However, there is that other 1 percent of the time when sentence fragments can make the sound you want. Here is an example.

> This lunatic called on Friday and told my answering machine that I would be dead by the end of the month. He called again on Saturday. Same message. After the third call I was worried. Real worried.

Those sentence fragments draw meaning from the sentences near them, and they create a nice rhythm by using fewer words than a complete sentence. But you should use sentence fragments like those only when you are certain that you are getting something in return.

Don't Repeat Uncommon Words

If you use a common word like "and" or "her" or even "house" six times in a paragraph, nobody is going to notice.

But if you write "Jackson made several inflammatory remarks during the debate. The final resolution had an inflammatory effect on the nation," you will make a disturbing sound in the reader's head. When the reader hears that second "inflammatory" she will say to herself, "Hmm, I think I've heard that word recently." It will sound familiar and it will remind her that she is reading.

The repeated words don't even have to be that close together or in exactly the same form to disturb the reader. Listen for the disturbance in this paragraph.

> Jason was struck more than ever by Gloria's beauty. She sat across from him, smiling, and there was an incandescence about her that he had never seen before. Not with her, not with any woman.
>
> After dinner they went out on the patio where the band played some of the old songs they had both danced to years ago with different partners. From their table they could look out over the city at night, its incandescent splendor like a fireworks display frozen in space, and he was reminded once again that being in love can change your view of everything.

When you heard "incandescent" fifty-six words after "incandescence" you were reminded of the writer at work.

After you use a word like "inflammatory" or "incandescent" or "inelegant" or "moribund," you certainly don't have to retire it for the rest of the story, but generally several paragraphs should pass before the reader hears it again, unless you are obviously repeating it for effect, such as, "Jackson's remarks were inflammatory. Wilson's remarks were inflammatory. In fact, everybody's remarks were inflammatory."

Put Emphatic Words at the End

Emphasis tends to flow to the end of a sentence, so if there is one word or phrase you want to say a little louder, put it at the end.

If there's been some confusion about which day the writer's workshop will be held, you can best remind people by putting the day at the end of the sentence:

> The writer's workshop, featuring guest speaker Ken Lizotte, will be held on Saturday.

If you want to emphasize the guest speaker you write:

> The writer's workshop on Saturday will feature guest speaker Ken Lizotte.

And if you want to emphasize what is happening on Saturday you write:

> Saturday Ken Lizotte will be the guest speaker at the writer's workshop.

This business of emphasis flowing to the end of the sentence is particularly important when you are trying to be funny. Often a writer loses the humor in his sentence by putting the funny word or phrase in the wrong place, where it loses emphasis. Woody Allen is the master of getting the funniest elements in his sentences to the end, where the reader will automatically emphasize them. The lines in this first set are just the way he wrote them, with the right words placed carefully at the end.
From "The UFO Menace":

> They told me they were from another galaxy and were here to tell the earth that we must learn to live in peace or they will return with special weapons and laminate every first-born male.

From "My Speech to the Graduates":

> No citizen can be wantonly tortured, imprisoned, or made to sit through certain Broadway shows.

From "By Destiny Denied":

> The store is an instant success, and by 1850 Entwhistle is wealthy, educated, respected, and cheating on his wife with a large possum.

In this second set I take the humorous element and move it up. Because you come to it sooner it is less emphatic, and less funny.

> They told me they were from another galaxy and would return with special weapons and laminate every first-born male if the earth did not learn to live in peace.

No citizen can be made to sit through certain Broadway shows, wantonly tortured, or imprisoned.

The store is an instant success, and by 1850, when Entwhistle is cheating on his wife with a large possum, he is wealthy, educated, and respected.

This lesson is best learned by ear. When you read your work, listen to how the impact in a sentence moves to whatever information happens to be at the end.

Listen

Always listen carefully to what you have written. Listen to your stories the way you would listen to a band rehearsal, or to your car's engine on a long trip. Is something out of tune, off the beat? Is something clanging that shouldn't be? In writing, there are no intrinsically good or bad sounds. Just as giggling is a "good" sound during recess and a bad sound during a geography test, the sound of your words must be considered in the context of what you have written.

Read your writing aloud. When you write and rewrite and constantly rearrange information, your ear for the sound of the written word becomes corrupted. Reading out loud will return to you the true sound of your story. You will hear the sour note of the word that's "just not right." The drastic changes in tone will call out to you for editing. You'll notice that you are breathless at the end of one long sentence and you will know that you must break it up into two or three. Listen for the music, the variety, the emphasis. You will discover that some of your sentences could be taken two different ways and that a single word or even a comma can eliminate the wrong one. And you will see that a sentence like "Who knew that Lou cued Sue, too?" might not look funny, but it sure makes a funny and distracting noise in the reader's head.

If you feel as if you are losing your ear for what you have written, try reading it out loud in sounds, not words. You might hear a sound that you don't like. If that doesn't work, put the manuscript away for a few days and then read it out loud, possibly with another listener. But before you do any of these things, go back and reread the tips in this chapter. They will help you to write well and that's always a sound idea.

FIVE

Imagery

In a sense, all of your writing can be called imagery. When I want you to see a dog I don't grab a cocker spaniel and paste him to the page. Instead, I draw a combination of lines that look like this: dog. And you see the animal. Imagery means the use of an image to represent something, rather than the thing itself.

In writing, imagery means the creation of one image to stand in for another image, or a series of other images, or a concept that cannot be explained without imagery.

The important thing about imagery, as we discuss it, is that it is representational. "The bull walked into a china shop" is not imagery, because you are saying there really is a bull and a china shop. "The man was like a bull in a china shop" is imagery because you are using the images of a bull and a china shop to show us something else, the clumsiness of a man.

Why Do We Use Imagery?

There are a lot of reasons why we use imagery in our writing. Sometimes the right image creates a mood we want. Sometimes an image can suggest connections between two things. Sometimes an image can make a transition smoother. We use images to show intention. *(Her words were fired in a deadly monotone and she gunned down the three of us with her smile.)* We use imagery to exaggerate. *(His arrival in that old Ford always sounded like a six-car pileup on the Harbor Freeway.)* Sometimes we don't know why we are using imagery; it just feels right. But the two main reasons we use imagery are:

1. To save time and words.
2. To reach the reader's senses.

By working with familiar images that are already implanted in the reader's mind we can save ourselves from long explanations.

Take, for example, Martin's blind date with Gloria last night. When Gloria greeted him at the door her face fell because she, apparently, was expecting someone more handsome, and perhaps taller. During dinner his explanation of how umbrella handles are made just seemed to bore her. And when he tried to charm her with humor she told him that she really didn't like crude and stupid jokes. At the door when he tried to kiss her goodnight, she turned her face away and he ended up kissing her barrette.

All of that is what happened. But when Martin tells you about it, he doesn't want to go into all the details. He wants to show you that he failed with Gloria, but since his failure is spread over a long period and several events, he searches his mind for an image that will compress failure into an instant. He thinks about a baseball player, whose failure occurs in the fraction of a second that it takes for the third strike to whiz past his bat. Martin says, "Last night I struck out with Gloria," and we all know what he means. That's using imagery to save time.

We also use imagery to make things that are not sensate, sensate. Something is sensate when it can be perceived by the senses. That is, it can be seen, heard, touched, smelled, or tasted. If it cannot be seen, heard, touched, etc., it is not sensate. Readers respond much better to the sensate, and so imagery helps us translate the abstract, the vague, the amorphous, into the concrete, easily understood world of the senses. For example, a common visual image for the abstract feeling of being in love would be, "He felt as if he were floating on a cloud." A sound image for the same thing could be, "He heard trumpets play whenever she approached him."

If you can't describe your character's feelings of nausea, use sight, touch, and taste and say, "Montgomery felt as if he had swallowed a seat cushion."

If Montgomery is depressed and you can't find words to get that feeling across you might use the image of a black bag thrown over his head, or a pane of glass slipped between him and reality. If he is elated he might feel as if he has a new engine. If he is confused, his mind might be like a junkyard.

Much of the imagery that we use is so common in writing and in speech that we don't even think of it as imagery. That is, we don't translate it; we accept it literally. For example, instead of describing all the mistakes and bad luck that plagued a man's job over a period of months we say, "His career went down the drain." Instead of describing the way the Celtics outscored the Philadelphia 76ers in every period of the game, we say, "The Celtics buried the Sixers yesterday, 140 to 97."

In a little while we'll talk about how to come up with images that work well, and how to avoid the ones that don't. But first I want to clarify a few of the terms which are used for certain types of imagery.

Symbolism

All imagery is symbolism. The baseball player striking out is a symbol for failure, and so forth. But symbolism is a word that is used so often by high school English teachers that you might have gotten the idea that it's important. It's not. Do you remember those stupid questions at the end of stories you read in junior year English? Things like, "What was the parrot a symbol of?" Well, nine times out of ten the parrot was a symbol of a parrot and the poor dead author had no idea that an English teacher would ask such a silly question two hundred years after the story was written.

In real life, professional writers don't spend much time thinking up symbols to put in their stories and articles. Symbols tend to occur naturally. Usually they are not something that a writer puts in. They are something that a reader takes out. The reader is, after all, a partner in the creation of the story. When you write a profile of the Senator from Nebraska who has become a presidential contender you might mention the bridge he crossed, driving into New Hampshire six months before the primary election, only because there happened to be a bridge there when you were talking to him. To your reader that bridge might be a symbol of the senator's crossing from the safe world of his Senate seat to the risky world of running for higher office. If it's a symbol for the reader, then it's a symbol, whether you intended it to be or not.

There are, of course, times when you will deliberately put something symbolic into your work, but even then it is not enough just to have it. You must use it. A symbol that is doing nothing except hanging around being a symbol will draw too much attention to itself and the reader will be distracted by the thought, "Gee, I wonder what that's a symbol for?"

Do you remember that previously in the Unity chapter I talked about "Streams," a short story based on chapter four of *Good If It Goes*, a book my wife Gail and I wrote for children? Well, in that chapter the stream is certainly a symbol for the Jewish people. But it is not isolated from the story. It is there specifically so that Max Levene, the grandfather, can use it as imagery.

> For a while we didn't say anything. We sat by the stream. I kept picking up twigs and breaking them in half, as if that would do any good. And Grampa just looked kind of peaceful the way he does when he's thinking.
>
> Finally, Grampa spoke.
>
> He lifted his hands a little bit and he said, "You see the stream, David. The traditions are like a stream, too, a stream that flows through the generations of Jewish people. You don't do this bar mitzvah for God, my grandson, you do it for your people in the past and in the future. It is the tradition, and the Hebrew language of your haftorah is the tradition also and that is what makes the Jewish people who they are. If there's no tradition there's no people."
>
> "Eddie Gould is not getting bar mitzvahed," I said. It was a pretty stupid thing to think of but I didn't know what else to say.
>
> "Then that is why you should," Grampa said.
>
> "Huh?"
>
> "When a boy does not have his bar mitzvah or when we do not light the candles on Chanukah or we do not eat the matzo at Passover, it is like throwing a twig into the stream. One twig, David, will not hurt your people. It will float away. Like our sins. But if you throw a twig and I throw a twig and Eddie Gould throws a twig, and everybody throws a twig, do you know what will happen?"

"The stream will stop." I said.

"Right, my grandson," Max Levene said.

That scene is an example of a symbol being used by the writers, but it's also a symbol being used by one of the characters. If we had created a scene later where David had gone and sat by the stream, the symbol would have served as shorthand for everything Max had said. But if we had written three or four more scenes with streams in them, the reader would have been too aware of the symbolism, and the effect would be the same as a cliché, where the reader becomes aware of the writer at work. So if you use symbols, don't overdo it.

In any case, symbolism is not something you have to give a lot of thought to. If something comes easily to you, fine. But if you find yourself trying to dream up symbols, don't use them.

I think one reason symbols emerge so often in the reading process is that writers do a good deal of their work subconsciously. *Good If It Goes,* for example, is the story of a boy preparing for his bar mitzvah. When a Jewish boy has a bar mitzvah it is said that he has become a man. Gail and I named our boy David Newman as in "new man." That seems like a pretty obvious symbol, but the truth is we never noticed that connection until after we had written the book.

Similes

You are using a simile when you say that one thing was like something that it's really very different from, usually to show some common quality. If you said that the pen in the gossip columnist's hand was like a pencil because it was made of wood and had an eraser, that would not be a simile. That would just be a handy way of describing the pen. But if you said that the pen was like a dagger, which he used to slice up the reputations of Hollywood's biggest stars, that would be simile. A pen is not really like a dagger at all, but you have made that connection to achieve a strong image for the reader.

Many similes have become clichés. The wise man is like an owl, the clever man is like a fox. The bad news hits him like a ton of bricks, and when he's feeling good he drinks and dances like there's no tomorrow. The word "like" is the tipoff that you have written a simile. Try to create some similes for these:

A boss who is grouchy.

A truck that won't start.

A pair of shoelaces that are almost broken in several places.

A wrinkled suit.

A woman who is too loud.

A book that is 1,200 pages long.

A trial that was much shorter than everybody expected.

A cigar that is annoying several people in a restaurant.

A flag that is old and dirty.

A piggy bank that has been smashed open.

Metaphors

Author Ted Cheney says that the difference between a simile and a metaphor is that the simile admits to being a figure of speech. That's a good explanation. The simile has "like" in it; the metaphor does not. In a metaphor we say that something *is* something else. We say that a woman's life was a river which meandered across the countryside, never rushing, never overflowing. We say that Herman and Rebecca's marriage was a war, and today Herman was on the offensive, storming Rebecca's fragile barriers.

Metaphors tend to be longer than similes. The woman who is like a river might have a "placid surface." She may "nourish everything that came to her shores." The couple at war may "shoot each other with words" or "call a truce." You are carrying on the metaphor for as long as you pretend that a woman is a river, a marriage is a war, or that anything is something else.

What Works and What Doesn't?

There are other terms for some of the types of imagery writers use, but I won't go into them here. The best discussion of them can be found on pages 172-184 of Ted Cheney's *Getting the Words Right* (Writer's Digest Books). Here I've just covered a few of imagery's terms to make sure you are clear on what imagery is. Now we can talk about what sort of imagery does or does not succeed in satisfying readers.

This is a tough lesson to teach. The experienced writer recognizes ineffective imagery when she sees it, but she can't always explain what's wrong with it. However, there are several types of ineffective imagery which can be described, and by exploring them, perhaps we can get a better general sense of what works and what doesn't.

Cliché Imagery

Earlier, when I gave you a list of similes, I said that many of them had become clichés. That is true for imagery in general. Here are some examples from manuscripts I have read.

> When he kissed her it was the fourth of July, fireworks exploding all around her, and bells ringing.
>
> He was broad shouldered, and the muscles on his stomach were like a washboard.
>
> When he awoke the morning after the party, Harriman felt as if his head had been stuffed with cotton.

Those images are not inappropriate. They are not far-fetched. The problem with them is that they are clichés. They have been used so often that your reader has probably seen them several times before. So when she sees them in your work she will be reminded that she is reading. She will see the writer at work.

Look at the imagery you have used and ask yourself, "Is this mine? Did I make it up? Did I really think about it? Or did I merely mimic something I had heard or read someplace else?" Examine each image and ask yourself where it is coming from. If it is not coming from you, get rid of it.

Extended Imagery

Just as many jokes that are hilarious in fifty words bomb miserably at a hundred words, many images won't work unless they are compacted into few words. Writers often invent interesting images, but destroy the effect by spreading the image too thin.

Consider this:

> With his second-hand Remington portable in front of him and the urge to write a novel burning inside of him, Brandy Firth began to explore his inner world. At first apprehensively, later with confi-

dence, he followed the trail of each ambition that dwelled within him until he came to a clearing. He climbed the mountains of his fears until he could stand atop each one and look for miles. He pushed back the thickets of confusion, hacking away with a machete of common sense. Each day he mapped out some new inner territory, which he would navigate alone. He felt like a pioneer crossing areas that had never been seen before. From time to time he was ambushed by some anxiety he hadn't known was there, and when he tried to pull back his wagon, the horses would often become confused and begin galloping desperately across years of memories that had been hidden behind a range, or forgotten on some barren prairie. He brought few supplies on these forays into his emotional wilderness, just his faith, and his curiosity and . . .

You get the idea. The imagery of the inner self as territory for exploration works okay. And the overall image is acceptable to the reader for several sentences. But as the writer continued with the image it became exaggerated and then ridiculous. The writer simply overdid it.

It is important that imagery not seem to be more important than the thing it stands for. If you say that Clarissa's smile was like the sunrise, then you've given us a nice sense of her smile in a few words. But if you say that her smile was like the sun rising over a long green meadow in spring, when the birds are singing and the air is still cool over the damp grass, etc., etc., the sunrise takes center stage and the smile is forgotten.

Images Too Similar

The cheetah ran like a gazelle.

What's wrong with that image is that it only repeats what the reader would have had in mind, anyhow—an animal with speed and grace. The image is too similar to the thing it is standing in for. Imagery has got to bring new information to bear on the thing it stands for. It has to give the reader a new way of looking at things. If it just repeats his old way of looking at information, then it is doing no work.

If you write an article on ice hockey and you say that being at a hockey game is like being at a football game, you haven't created any fresh imagery. You've only transferred the same images: competition, a crowd, the smell of hot dogs, etc. The reader doesn't know any more than he would know without the imagery. But if you say that being at a hockey game is like being at a prize fight, then you have created an image concerning the violence in hockey. You've suggested that in hockey a fight is the main event, that the crowd likes to see the punching, that there is a certain amount of bloodlust, perhaps even some betting on the outcome of fights. The imagery brings something new to the hockey game.

Reaching for Images

Imagery should appear to come naturally. If your image is so specific or so remote that the reader becomes aware of it as an image, he will also be aware of you as a writer and the imagery won't work.

Listen to what happens in your mind when you hear these images.

The buttons on Doris's coat were small and square like the little gray buttons you use to store telephone numbers on one of those new phones with built-in computers.

Tish was much smaller than her sisters, like a xylem cell that had been produced in the latter part of the year.

Those images are too obviously the work of a writer sweating over a typewriter. The writer who reaches that far to come up with an image will be as obtrusive as the dinner guest who reaches all the way across the table for the salt shaker.

Mixed Imagery

Generally, a collection of disparate images close together on the page will not work. At best, they will have the effect of sketching on the reader's mind a writer dreaming up images. At worst they will make you look like a buffoon.

An example of this would be the mixed metaphor:

Her love life had long been a desert on which nothing grew until she met Ted Ross and the waves of passion carried her to a shore she had never even seen before.

Here, we begin by saying that her love life is a desert and we end up saying it is an ocean. That's a mixed metaphor. Once you enter a metaphor you must be true to it until you have left it. There is nothing wrong with using the desert metaphor in chapter one and the ocean metaphor in chapter six, but if you mix them or even use them within a few para-

graphs of each other, they will be disturbing and, perhaps, unintention-
ally amusing.

The same goes for similes, though the reader can be a little more
forgiving. You could use two, sometimes even three, different similes
close together, but don't push your luck beyond that. For example, in
the Pace chapter of this book, I compared unnecessary words to "luggage" at one point and to "junk" at another. You allowed me that, I
hope. But if I had also said that unnecessary words were "like garbage," and a few paragraphs later "like handcuffs," and later "like an-
chors," the chapter would begin to sound like a comedy routine.

Think About Qualities

In trying to come up with good imagery for your stories, don't make the
mistake of thinking literally. An apple is literally like a pear. Both have
roughly the same shape and weight, they both grow on trees, they are
both fruit, both edible, both juicy, etc. But one would not work as an image for the other. You would have more luck saying that an apple has the
heft of a baseball, the color of a lady's cheek, or that it dangled from the
branch like a Christmas bulb.

Imagery is not merely an attempt to show something more clearly.
It's an attempt to say something specific about that thing, such as
"Hockey is a violent sport." Do not use imagery until you know what it
is you are trying to say, and then choose an image that has the quality
which will best convey that message.

Now let's take, for example, a cornfield and apply some imagery.

If you wrote, "The corn was as high as an elephant's eye" the
reader might recognize that as a line from a Broadway song, and the effect would be of a cliché, unless the reader thought you were specifically alluding to the song.

If you wrote, "The rows of corn were as straight as the lines on a
seersucker suit," you would be reaching for an image which would distract the reader. It would not work.

If you wrote, "The cornfield was a wheat field waiting to be harvested," you would create a metaphor so similar to the thing it is standing in for that the reader would be totally confused.

If you wrote, "The rows of corn were like soldiers standing at attention," you would succeed in showing certain qualities of cornstalks,
the erectness, the stillness. If the corn had been beaten in all directions

by a windstorm you might change the simile to "soldiers in combat," to show the wreckage, the disarray. If the corn had been picked, the stalks might be compared to something naked to show that quality.

And you would be mixing your images if you wrote, "The corn had been harvested. Like pennant hopes it would be planted again next spring, but for now a chapter had ended."

Identification

One of my favorite novels is Dan Wakefield's *Under the Apple Tree*. There is no resistance to Wakefield's prose, no bumps or rough spots. I hated to see the book end. I found *Under the Apple Tree* exciting, touching, and compelling, so it might surprise you to learn that the novel had virtually no sex, murders, suicides, divorces, terrorist attacks, counterspies, or secret pasageways. It's a simple story about a twelve-year-old boy on the homefront during World War II.

Why would any reader care about a twelve-year-old boy doing ordinary things?

The answer is "identification."

Artie Garber, Wakefield's twelve-year-old hero, lives in a small Illinois town. The war is on and Artie worries a lot about an invasion. So he helps out. He goes up on roofs to watch for German planes.

Now, as adult readers we know that no German planes invaded any small Illinois town, and that such a thing was unlikely. We know that what Artie is doing is unimportant. So why do we climb to the roof with him?

Because it's important to him.

Why do we watch for German planes when we know they are not coming?

Because he doesn't know that.

We get Artie's feelings of exhilaration, his fears, his hopes, and his triumphs through reading, because we identify with him. We pretend that we are him.

Let's take another book I read recently, *The Bridge Across Forever* by Richard Bach. Bach is a wonderful writer who believes in soul mates and predestination, and those beliefs are integral to the book. To me they are as meaningless as tarot cards, and yet I was enthralled by the book. Why?

Identification.

It's not important that I agree with Bach about finding a soul mate.

I'm not a Catholic either, but one of my favorite novels is about a priest trying to find his proper place in the church. What's important in the Bach book is what he believes in and that his beliefs fuel his writing in a way that makes me feel what he feels. I can feel like me anytime. We read so that we can feel like somebody else for a while. That's what identification is.

What does this mean to you? It means you don't have to always write about "important" things like war or politics or multinational conglomerates. You can write about a girl's wish that a certain boy will call for a date, or the thousands of people who are changing professions in midlife, or the process of making friends. The issues in your book or story don't have to be important to the world. They just have to be important to the fictional character or real person with whom the reader identifies.

Identification is important to the writer in another way, before he begins to write.

Take, for example, *The Blaspheming Moon,* a book by Christopher Hewitt.

The Blaspheming Moon is an imagined diary of the artist Achille Emperaire. Emperaire is an important and interesting artist, but let's face it, you probably never heard of him and neither did I until I came upon the book. Which leads us to the question, "Why would anybody want to write a book about an artist that few people have heard of?"

Christopher Hewitt suffers from a congenital bone condition called osteogenesis imperfecta. He has bones that can fracture, he writes, "like the snapping of green bamboo or a stick of celery." As a result, Hewitt views life from a wheelchair. Achille Emperaire also suffered from osteogenesis imperfecta, though, unlike Hewitt, he could walk with a cane. When Hewitt first saw a portrait of Emperaire, he was, he says, "shocked by the striking resemblance between Emperaire and myself." That's when Hewitt began to research, and learned about the disability.

So Christopher Hewitt wrote a book about a little-known artist because he identifies with him. And it's a pretty good reason. The men lived in different centuries, in different countries, but they have a bond, a shared experience, the experience of living with a specific disability.

In his introduction Hewitt writes, "The physical similarity between Emperaire and myself is merely the pretext for my writing the book and has little to do with the subject matter." This is true. It is the inner similarity that has everything to do with the book.

So if you want to write about anybody, whether he is a real person or a fictitious character, search for that level on which you identify with your subject. Find the shared experience, whether it is suffering, jubilation, or anything in between and write from there, because your understanding of the character springs from that shared experience.

PART
TWO

Originality

Samuel Johnson, a man not known for beating around the bush, once told a writer, "Your manuscript is both good and original, but the part that is good is not original and the part that is original is not good."

As a writer you are a technician, but you are also a creative artist and if you forget that word "creative" you will be wasting paper every time you sit down to write. In your writing, all of the parts should be good and many of them should be original. Your reader doesn't expect everything you write to be a news flash, but he does expect to find in your writing something he has never heard before.

For everything you write you should be able to answer the question, "How is this different from similar pieces of writing?" Does this mean that you can't write that diet article, or that you can't write a profile of Mary Tyler Moore, because these things have been done before? Not at all. Being original doesn't mean you have to invent a totally new idea every time you want to write an article or a chapter in a book. As I noted in my introduction, much of the advice in *Make Every Word Count* is repeated in this book. I just present it in a different way with different examples, and in the context of a different book.

Most good ideas are published hundreds of times and some, like "You Can Lose Weight by Going on a Diet," are published hundreds of times *every month*. Some romance publishers, it could be argued, publish the same book six times every month under different titles. But those books sell by the truckload because the readers find something unique in each one. Being original means you find new slants, creative leads, fresh information, unique formats, different ways of looking at old information, surprising conclusions, and imaginative solutions. Being original is an attitude that you bring to your work.

If you are writing magazine articles, you could bring originality to the piece by using a different format, such as writing the article as if it were a newscast. Or you might write it from a surprising point of view, perhaps writing about a celebrity the way his child would see him. But usually you bring originality to an article with your choice of slant, your fresh way of approaching the subject.

Let me give you an example. I've written several writer profiles for *Writer's Digest* magazine. In some ways the articles all had to be shaped by the same cookie cutter. They were roughly the same length, they all had to carry a lot of quotes, and each had to be filled with information that would be useful and entertaining to writers. If I hadn't tried to find original ways to approach each profile, they would have all looked the same. I would have gotten bored at the typewriter and the reader would have felt as if he'd read the article before.

Of course, I wasn't free to do just anything in the name of originality. Whatever I did had to be compatible with the magazine's requirements. I couldn't, for example, write, "What Janet Dailey Does in Her Spare Time," or "William Styron's Ten Favorite Recipes for Christmas Duckling." I had to be original within the requirements of the piece.

When I interviewed Ellen Goodman I observed that her great success, which had recently been rewarded with a Pulitzer Prize, came because her readers had the feeling "she thinks like me." And so I decided that an original angle for my Ellen Goodman piece would be to somehow insert one of those readers into the story. But this was for *Writer's Digest* so I wanted not just a person who thinks like Goodman, but a writer . . . someone who dreamed of becoming an Ellen Goodman. I chose my friend Linda Dolan, a rookie writer and a Goodman fan. While meeting all the requirements of the magazine, I built my story around the relationship between these two women who have never met.

"Sometimes I think Ellen Goodman is tapping my phone," Linda once told me. "She says so many of the things in print that I'd like to say."

While Linda understands that Ellen Goodman would be out of business tomorrow if millions of other fans weren't saying exactly the same thing, on another level Linda, like those others, suspects that Goodman is speaking directly to her.

Later I ask Ellen Goodman about this in a tiny windowless storeroom at the *Globe* where we have gone to tape an interview and escape from the clacking of typewriters.

"I've thought about this a lot," she says, pausing to think about it some more. At thirty-nine she is more youthful than the well-seasoned oracle one would expect to produce such wise and authoritative columns. She smiles often when she speaks, and her eyes get wide and her hands brush through the air as if to clear away all previous thoughts.

"What I think happens," she says, "is that I respond the same way they respond. I mean I look at something like the Eleanor Roosevelt letters flap, for example, and I say 'Yuk.' And they look at it and they say, 'Yuk.' My job is to say why yuk. News is divided into stories that tell you what happened and stories that tell you what it means. I am paid to figure out what it means. I face the world with as much confusion as everybody else, but once in a while it's nice to figure out what I think a few things mean."

And what about Linda Dolan out in Shrewsbury, stubbornly lugging her typewriter to the kitchen table every morning? With two kids to raise and a husband who comes home hungry, can she ever hope to write in the same league as Ellen Goodman?

The article goes on like that, interweaving the accomplishments of Ellen Goodman and the aspirations of Linda Dolan. Between the lines I am expressing the view that each woman symbolizes the reason for the other's success. That's what makes the piece original.

Take Risks

When I wrote another of those author profiles, on novelist Dan Wakefield, my slant was to show the reader all the steps I was taking in writing the article. I told the reader what material I had read about Wakefield before I met him, how I contacted him, what notes I jotted down while talking to him, and so forth. I assumed the reader who was interested in writers would also be interested in how this writer went about writing the article about the writer.

When I wrote the piece I had a sickening hunch that my editor would take one look at it and say, "Just who does this bozo think he is, writing about *his* research and *his* questions and *his* notes? Who gives a damn?" The entire editorial office would have a good howl about my "original approach," ha, ha, and then the pages, stained with tears of laughter, would come back to me with a note that said, "Gary, pretend you are a normal human being and rewrite this."

That's the thing about being original. It's a lot like walking across the street at noon. It's risky. You always think you've come up with something fresh that works, but as soon as you drop the manuscript in the mail box a pixie elf lights on your shoulder and whispers in your ear, "You've just made a fool of yourself, you know that, don't you?"

But you have no choice. If you don't take chances in your writing you will perish as a writer, or you will become an alcoholic writer who can't understand why he never got anywhere with the writing.

Look at every line you write as an opportunity to embarrass yourself or to prove what a genius you are. In your early drafts, startle the reader with some shocking leads, pepper the page with powerful words that might not even mean what you think they mean, include bizarre metaphors and surprising analogies, write flowery prose that might make you blush later, mix the plaids with the stripes. Live dangerously. Later you can put on the safety belt, but don't pull it too tightly. In the second or third draft you can cut the inappropriate, the distracting; you can look up those powerful words in the dictionary and deport the ones that don't belong; you can chop out all the things that just don't work. Nobody ever has to know what a jerk you were. But if you're too cautious to begin with they'll never know what a marvelous writer you are.

Think Original

Being unoriginal is a bad habit, and soon we will be discussing the ways in which that bad habit shows up in manuscripts.

You can break that bad habit by exercising your mind. You are a writer. You probably have a treasure chest full of creativity just waiting to be hauled up from deep in your subconscious. Before we go on to some specific ways you can bring originality to your work, try these exercises. They will help you to get that creativity up to the surface.

1. Think of three uses for a coat hanger on a golf course.
2. Think of a way to feed your dog when he's alone in the house for two days.
3. Think of five more exercises that are like the two above.
4. In 250 words, describe the inside of a Ping-Pong ball.
5. Find something that you wrote before you read this chapter and replace every adjective and verb, even if the new ones don't make sense.

Clichés and Word Packages

Being original doesn't mean you have to constantly concoct word combinations that have never been used before. That would be impossible. I often use phrases that I've read elsewhere; I have phrases of my own that I use frequently; and, I hope, I've written phrases that other writers have installed in their own work.

But being original does mean that each sentence should smell fresh when it arrives in front of the reader. If the reader has seen your sentence before, it should look as though it has been reinvented, not pulled off of a shelf in the sentence warehouse.

There are hundreds of sentences and phrases which have been used so many times that they will never again smell fresh. They are clichés like "cute as a button" and "avoid it like the plague." Your first step in "thinking original" is to excise these clichés from your writing.

Clichés land on your manuscript page when you are too lazy to think, or too timid to take a chance.

You didn't take the time to visualize how the governor might have gotten rid of his new aide, Peterson, when the press revealed that Peterson was a child molester, so you wrote, "When the story hit the front page of the *Times Picayune,* the governor dropped Peterson like a hot potato."

You thought of some clever ways to describe your character's dumbness, but you thought they looked silly, so you played it safe and said, "Clarence was dumb as a doornail."

Review your manuscripts. Look at each sentence, each phrase. Do you really feel as if you made up that combination of words, or at least reinvented it? Or is it something that was hanging there in the air for everybody to see and anybody to grab? Is it fresh or is it stale? Is it something that you and your readers have read a thousand times? Get rid of it. Replace it with something original. I once crossed out "as useless as a refrigerator to an Eskimo" and changed it to "as useless as a pair of inflatable paperweights." I'm not sure if that's good, but I know it's mine.

What would you change these to?

1. He was as wise as an owl.
2. She was as meek as a lamb.
3. She was a pretty, blue-eyed blonde.
4. He was tall, dark, and handsome.

Closely related to clichés are something called "word packages." The novelist Anne Bernays told me that the use of word packages is one of the most common mistakes of her writing students, so I'll let her tell you about them.

"They are somewhere between a cliché and a noncliché," Anne said, "They are verbal formulas that come very quickly to you and you just put them down. For example, a woman in my class wrote, 'I walked the two long blocks to her house.' 'Two long blocks' is a word package. It's easy to say and she thinks she's saying something, but she's not. Were they really two long blocks? Were they longer than any other blocks, or did they just seem longer because she was in a hurry or anxious? Other word packages would be 'by all rights' or 'I felt curiously tired.' They don't mean anything."

Anne, incidentally, admits that she uses word packages in her first and second drafts. That's okay. We all do. First drafts don't have to smell fresh; final drafts do. Go through your manuscript and cut out those phrases that don't mean anything.

Original Description

If you are inclined to use clichés and word packages, you are probably writing description that sounds as if it came off a shelf. A lot of dull description comes from those clichés and word packages, and especially from the overuse of stock phrases that the writer types into his manuscript without even noticing that he didn't make anything up.

The key to coming up with original description is to STOP and THINK.

Sometimes your story needs a cop to come to the door so, without even thinking about it, you write, "A burly policeman came to the door."

This is the time to stop and think.

Does this police officer have to be burly? Did you even stop to think about what burly means? Walk to that door. Open it. Take a good look. There is an individual policeman there, not a clone of fifty that you saw on television last month. Is he really burly, or is he slight? Does he wear eyeglasses? Does he have red hair? Maybe he is a she. Imagine this person off duty, wearing street clothes. Now put the uniform back on. What do you see? Describe it.

The same thing with places. Maybe you want your teenaged boy to find a canvas bag full of stolen money buried on the beach. Automatically you make it a sunny day with the smell of salt in the air and waves rushing to an uncluttered shore. Because that's the way beaches are in the stock descriptions that have been etched into your mind. That's fine for some beaches. But is that what you really want, or are you just not thinking? There are rainy days on the beach, too, and you can't always smell the salt, and quite often the shore is littered with seaweed or that other disgusting stuff that looks like knots of dead snakes.

There's nothing wrong with a beach that has a blue sky and sunshine, but make sure it's *your* blue sky and *your* sunshine. The point is, think. Put yourself on that beach. Don't just mimic all the other beach descriptions. *Experience it for yourself.* It is the skinny, red-headed police officer and the cloudy day at the beach that make your writing believable.

In writing nonfiction, even though you usually have seen or experienced what you are describing, it's easy to slip into the habit of typing stock description unless you really look at what you are seeing. You are not just describing what you see. You are describing *how* you see it. And if you don't make your own observation, you'll be making somebody else's.

I once interviewed Bobby Riggs, the tennis player. It would have been easy to repeat the stock description of him as a cocky male chauvinist. But I wanted to see him with my own eyes. So before I interviewed him for a while I watched him operate in the lounge of a tennis club. The image that came to my mind was of a whirlwind, a little storm, and that's how I described him at the beginning of my article.

> Bobby Riggs has a way of storming into a town. It's the way he's come into hundreds of towns since his gravy days of playing Margaret Court and Billie Jean King.

> He arrives, all noise and motion, a little wound up munchkin of a man tossing Sugar Daddies, signing autographs, ribbing the gals, and grinning behind his eyeglasses because people still rush to pump his hand.

> He still craves action and attention. He's still an admiration junkie and if he can't get it on television in front of 40 million people, he'll get his fixes one or two at a time in places like Westboro.

Anne Bernays, the novelist who talked about word packages, said something else to me which I think is particularly appropriate in a discussion of description.

"I've learned," Anne said, "that nice writing isn't enough. It isn't enough to have smooth and pretty language. You have to surprise the reader frequently; you can't just be nice all the time. Provoke the reader. Astonish the reader. Writing that has no surprises is as bland as oatmeal. Surprise the reader with the unexpected verb or adjective. Use one startling adjective per page."

I smiled at her and she knew what I was thinking. The word "startling" had surprised me. It was a startling adjective.

I have found this tip very helpful. When I write I try to keep that word "startling" in mind. I know I can't startle my reader with "a burly police officer." But a police officer who stutters or wears a hairpiece or a skirt . . . that will keep my reader interested.

Can you wake up your reader by making these unoriginal descriptions a little more startling?

1. The front of the store was a big shiny window and Freda saw her reflection in it.

2. We went to school in an old red brick building that was almost a block long.

3. Manute used to walk across the campus every morning bouncing a basketball. He was a tall black man, skinny as a string bean.

Stereotypes

A stereotype is to characterization what a cliché is to description. A stereotype character is one that your editor has seen almost as many times as he's seen his mother, and that character is another enemy of originality. When an editor tells you that your character is a stereotype, he means that instead of creating a living, breathing person, you have wheeled in a dummy from the stereotype warehouse, which is just two long blocks away from the cliché warehouse.

In the manuscripts that were sent to me last year I saw these stereotypes several times each:

The wise-cracking private detective who is hardboiled and cynical.

The sweet old schoolteacher who bakes cookies for everybody.

The innocent young girl in the big city who falls in love with Mr. Wonderful the first time she sees him.

The wise, handsome, and successful hero who falls in love with the innocent young girl in the big city the first time he sees her.

You get the idea. Perhaps you've hired a few of these mannequins to do work you were supposed to do.

Stereotypes are not confined to fiction. Even though the people in your nonfiction are real human beings, they are stereotypes if they don't show up on the page that way. Hollywood publicity was filled with stereotypes for years. The starlets all seemed to be the same virgin from a small town in Kansas. The handsome new leading man always seemed to share the same manly values as the last handsome new leading man. Today many of our less original sports writers always portray the hardworking, unsung utility infielder as if that's all there was to him. The nonfiction stereotype results when the writer takes a one-dimensional view of his subject, either because the writer hasn't really looked at that person, or because he's afraid to take chances.

An editor I know (who, incidentally, is not gruff, harried, or cynical) once told me that the most common problem with the profile articles he rejects is that the writer seems to have fallen in love with his subject. The person comes off as perfect, and that makes for a pretty boring article.

In fiction and nonfiction the stereotypical characters are always too something. The girls are too pretty, the men too handsome, the villains too cruel, the heroes too heroic, the politicians too corrupt, the vine-covered cottages too cozy, the director too talented, the children too adorable (as are the puppies), the little old ladies and ministers always too sweet.

Here is an example from one of my old manuscripts. It was to be a novel called *Spring Was Never Waiting*.

> Clay was a tall, good-looking guy who never left a female head unturned. He had lustrous dark hair, thick eyebrows, perfect teeth, and a friendly smile. He had the body of an Olympic gymnast and the quick, agile movements of a cat. His complexion was flawless and so were his manners. He moved with the confidence of a king. Clearly he was a man who was totally in control of his life, and perhaps the lives of many others.

Anytime you create a character who has "perfect" something, "flawless" something else, and is "totally" anything, go back and rethink it. Chances are you are creating a robot, not a person.

There's nothing wrong with these stereotypes as a starting point. You have to start somewhere. But look at a stereotype as the granite into which you chisel your individual and atypical character.

The character who emerges should be not quite like anybody else. He should be inconsistent, he should have good points and bad, strengths and weaknesses. There should be some surprises in his make-up.

One Way to Avoid Stereotypes

Here is an exercise that will help you to come up with original characters.

1. Imagine a character you want to write about. She can be a fictional character or a real person for a work of nonfiction. Give me a three-word description of that character, such as "a war hero" or "a retired schoolteacher."

2. Write three adjectives that would support a stereotype of that character—that is, three adjectives that the reader would assume if he knew nothing else about the character. For example, if you used "war hero," three adjectives in the stereotype would be "male, brave, patriotic" (even though she could be a cowardly anarchist).

3. Now tell me one thing that would shatter my assumptions. Tell me something true of your character that is not true of the stereotype. Perhaps your war hero *is* male, brave, and patriotic, but if you tell me that he also collects ceramic pigs I will begin to see him as an individual. When you do this, choose a trait that really is true of your character, not one you've thrown in just for the sake of making her different. The deliberate contrast, such as the homosexual football player, or the sweet old lady who is really an ax murderer, is itself a stereotype.

4. Think about how this quality might have gotten your character in trouble once, or gotten her out of it. How did it win her praise or bring her condemnation? How does she use it to manipulate people, or how do people use it to manipulate her?

5. Describe a scene in which you would reveal character through this trait.

6. Write the scene.

Now let's see how this sort of exercise might enrich a book. The book we will work with is Edwin O'Connor's famous novel, *The Last Hurrah.* The book's main character is Frank Skeffington, an aging Irish Catholic, Boston politician, a man who might easily have filled a stereotyper's mold. But in the hands of a fine writer, Skeffington came to life. He outgrew the book and stepped out of the pages and into the public consciousness, so that today he is known to many people who never read the book.

By the time I read page four of *The Last Hurrah,* O'Conner had convinced me that I was in the room with a flesh-and-blood Skeffington and that I knew the man well. Naturally, I went back to see how he had done it.

I found that O'Connor had created an eminently believable Frank Skeffington in the first chapter by working largely with one trait that was in the character, but not in the stereotype. That trait was Skeffington's love of reading.

On page one Skeffington is thinking about retirement, "far from the madding crowd," he says, using a literary allusion. When the reporters ask him what he would do in retirement, he answers, "Read."

And in the next few pages O'Connor shows us:

1. *What Skeffington reads:*

The reporter had been persistent. "Which great books?"

Skeffington's eyes had opened, the silver head had lifted, and once more the reporters met the deadpan look. "I don't know whether you'd know them or not," he had said thoughtfully. "The Bible, which is a book composed of two parts, commonly called the Old and the New Testaments. The poems and plays of Shakespeare, an Englishman."

2. *How Skeffington feels about reading:*

After breakfast he picked up a book and settled down by the long front bedroom window to read; this had been his morning custom for nearly fifty years. When his wife was alive, much of the time he had read aloud to her; for the last ten years he had read silently to himself. He read poetry for the most part, and he read chiefly for sound, taking pleasure in the patterns of words as they formed and echoed deep within his brain.

3. *How reading has influenced Skeffington's career:*

It was an incongruous picture: the aging political boss, up shortly after dawn, preparing for the daily war of the wards by reading a volume of verse; it was a picture from which Skeffington—who was capable, at times, of great detachment—derived considerable amusement. He knew that the widely publicized habit had given rise to indignation, even fury, among his opponents; in several campaigns it had cropped up as a major issue.

4. *How Skeffington's reading affected some other people:*

"Here we are in this grand city of ours, payin' the highest tax rate we've ever paid, and the garbage hasn't been collected for weeks," he would cry. "Our back yards are bein' turned into veritable *bedlams* of nauseous perfumes and where is the mayor while all this is goin' on? I'll tell you where he is; he's up in his mansion on the avenue, readin' *pomes!* The city smells to high heaven and Frank Skeffington's got his nose in a book!"

All of this emerges because perhaps one afternoon Edwin O'Connor placed a sheet of paper on his desk and labeled it "Skeffington's Character Traits." And then, pausing to think of just the right thing, he wrote, "Skeffington reads."

Don't Depend on Attributions

When a writer is being unoriginal it usually means that he is replacing creativity with dependence. In description he depends on clichés; in characterization he depends on stereotypes; and in plotting he often depends on "headlines," which I'll discuss shortly.

In dialogue the writer often shows his lack of originality by depending on attributions. Attributions are those phrases that show the reader who is speaking; that is, they attribute the words to somebody. Of course the reader needs to know who is speaking, but the problem is that the beginning writer too often also tells us how the speaker is speaking. In other words, he describes the dialogue.

The beginning writer becomes insecure about his dialogue. He's not sure that the reader can hear the tone of voice, understand the implication. He's afraid the reader won't "get it." So the writer drives his pickup truck down to the attribution warehouse and picks up two crates of overused attributions like "she intoned," "Thurgood asked quizzically," and "Fred queried." Figuring that the more he uses, the safer he'll be, the writer sets out to describe the dialogue he has written. One crate is full of verbs; the other is full of adverbs. With verbs, describing the dialogue looks like this:

"I'm not afraid of you," I announced.

"Oh," Joel snarled, "What are you going to do, scare me off with a song?"

"Maybe," I shot back.

"Or maybe you're going to hit me with a karate chop," he chided.

"Someday you'll be sorry," I muttered.

"When you least expect it," he threatened, "when you least expect it," which is what he always says to a kid he's planning to beat up.

In this case the variety of verbs (announced, threatened, chided, etc.) is distracting, silly sounding, and unnecessary. Once in a while a strong verb will give a line of dialogue a little extra punch, but usually when we know the characters and the situation we can hear the tone of voice without the writer interrupting the dialogue to tell us.

Here is how the same mistake would look with adverbs:

"I'm not afraid of you," I said quickly.

"Oh," Joel said sarcastically, "What are you going to do, scare me off with a song?"

"Maybe," I replied weakly.

"Or maybe you're going to hit me with a karate chop," he said derisively.

"Someday you'll be sorry," I meekly replied.

"When you least expect it," he hissed ominously, "when you least expect it."

The writer in this case thinks he's improving the dialogue by writing "sarcastically," "derisively," etc. In fact, he is robbing the dialogue of its impact and its spontaneity by constantly interrupting to explain how something was said.

That dialogue is from *Popcorn* (Bradbury Press), a children's novel which my wife and I wrote. But when we wrote the dialogue we didn't use any adverbs or any verbs, except *said*, a word which is so common and so easily understood that it sails right by without interrupting the dialogue.

When you write dialogue, use "said" or no verb at all most of the time. Rarely use adverbs to describe dialogue, and only when necessary. Dialogue that is original contains its own tone of voice. If you feel that a lot of your dialogue won't be understood unless you describe it, then perhaps the dialogue is not original; perhaps you are mimicking something you heard or read.

Coming Up with Original Dialogue

While many writers tend to repeat the clichés of description or the stereotypes of characterization, there is no such bugaboo common in dialogue. Certainly there are clichés of dialogue, usually lines from old movies, like, "Stop or I'll shoot," but they are not used often and they are not big contributors to the problem of unoriginality in dialogue.

The writer who is unoriginal in his dialogue is not usually repeating specific lines that he has heard a thousand times, but, rather, types of lines that he hears every day. Common conversation. He writes dialogue like:

"I've got to go to the post office," she said. She had a stack of letters in her hand.

"Are you going to your doctor's appointment now?" Richard asked.

"No," she said. "I'll stop back here first. I know how you like to see the mail. And I'll take Buster with me when I go. He's supposed to get a shot at the vet."

"Would you pick up some stamps while you're at the post office?" he asked, remembering the stack of unanswered letters on his desk.

This is ordinary everyday conversation, but it is not good dialogue. Good dialogue is not real speech. Good dialogue is the best of real speech, the most emotional, most tense, moments of real speech. Good dialogue is real speech's greatest hits.

The above dialogue could be made interesting by the addition of tension, and when we get to the chapter on tension I will give you a similar example and show you how to add tension to dialogue. But for now, let's not think about the fact that it lacks tension so much as the fact that it lacks originality. It is bland. It sounds like ordinary conversations that take place in your house every day. Original dialogue sounds like special conversations. The problem with the dialogue above is that the writer is just playing back an old tape recording in his mind, instead of creating a new conversation. To come up with original dialogue, do the same thing I said to do for original description. STOP and THINK.

Here are some of the things you should think about.

When you write dialogue do what an actor does. Get inside the character. Ask yourself, "What am I feeling at this moment in the scene?" Your dialogue will be much better if you stop to think about what the character is feeling before you write it. Is he angry? Is he sad? Is he hiding something? Is he happy?

Maybe when you stop to think about the above dialogue you decide that Richard is feeling deadline pressure from whatever work he is doing at his desk. Because he senses that time is short, he speaks no unnecessary words. You might change the dialogue:

"I've got to go to the post office," she said. She had a stack of letters in her hand.

"Doctor, too?" he asked.

"No," she said, "I'll stop back here first. I know how you like to see the mail. And I'll take Buster with me when I go. He's supposed to get a shot at the vet."

"Stamps, please," Richard said, remembering the stack of unanswered letters on his desk.

Or maybe you decide that it is the woman who is feeling harried. She's a little overwhelmed by all the things she's got to get done today.

"I suppose I'll have to go to the post office," she said. She held a stack of letters tightly in her hand.

"Are you going to your doctor's appointment now?" Richard asked.

"Oh God, the doctor! No, no, let me see, no, I'll come back here first. I can't let everything hold up the mail; you need it. Maybe I can save some time by taking Buster with me when I go. I can't believe he needs another shot at the vet already."

Obviously you could do a lot more than I have done in those examples, but I wanted to stay close to my first passage to make the point about originality. Think about what your characters are feeling and you will create words that will come from *their particular situation,* not from similar situations in general.

Another thing to think about is the overall tone of the dialogue scene. Sometimes the writer makes assumptions about the mood of a scene, and he can often come up with original dialogue by questioning and changing those assumptions.

For example, when your cop brings a murder suspect in for interrogation, do you automatically assume that the cop is hostile and domineering, and the suspect is resistant, that there is an adversarial relationship between them? What if you recast the scene with the idea that these two are businessmen negotiating? The cop wants information, the suspect wants freedom. Maybe they could be very civil to each other, either in a phony way or in a sincere way? That new premise doesn't have to change the outcome of the scene. The cop still finds out that the victim was a loan shark, or whatever. But the new premise creates a whole smorgasbord of original dialogue possibilities.

When I wrote *Finder* I had to write a dialogue scene in which Marilyn Greene announces at the dinner table that she has quit her job in order to pursue a career as a private investigator. As I originally wrote the scene the mood is one of antagonism. Chip, her husband, is angry with her for quitting. She gets angry with him. He gets angrier with her, and so forth. After I reread the dialogue I realized that it conveyed the same mood as several other scenes in which Marilyn and Chip had argued. To the reader it would feel like a scene he had read before, and because of that, the dialogue would sound unoriginal. So, to make the dialogue original, I reconsidered the mood of the scene. Instead of letting the dialogue build up to an argument with someone walking out or slamming a door, as they had in previous scenes, I decided I could accomplish the same work, but with fresher dialogue, if I introduce a humorous tone to the dialogue. Here's what I came up with.

"You can't just quit your job," Chip said.

"Sure I can."

"It's irresponsible," he said. "We need the money. What makes you think it will be so easy to get another job?"

"I've already got one."

"Oh, you're not going to start that stuff again about raising kids being a job. I know it's work, for God's sake, I do my share of it. But it doesn't pay."

"I'm a private investigator, remember?"

"Oh Jesus!"

"Oh Jesus, yourself," I said. "I can do it. I got my license, didn't I? I can specialize in finding missing persons."

"Oh, great," Chip said. "I'm sure there's a big call for that. I bet there's millions of missing persons right here in Albany, huh? Marilyn, get realistic. How many cases do you think you can get out of Albany, Schenectady, and Troy? Or did you think millionaires were going to call you from Palm Springs and say 'My wife's missing, can you get down here right away?' "

Chip liked to laugh at his own jokes, and now he was more amused by himself than he was angry with me. Soon the kids started giggling, and even though I knew I was the butt of the joke, I smiled. It was nice to see everyone happy.

"I called Benjamin Bragonier today," I said when the laughter died down. "He's the lawyer who advertises in the paper. He told me he gets plenty of business just in Albany and all he does is immigration cases."

"Ben Bragonier is a lawyer, for God's sake," Chip said. "You can't charge what lawyers charge."

"I suppose you're right," I said. "Gee, now that I think of it, I wonder what I should charge."

"Oh Jesus!" Chip said.

Avoid Unoriginal Endings

Because this is the end of the Originality chapter, it seems like a good time to discuss the lack of originality in endings. Nonfiction doesn't usually present the writer with difficulty in bringing the piece to the finish line. That's because in nonfiction, the writer has not created for himself a "problem" that must be solved. In fiction there is almost invariably a problem that must be solved, and the writer who hasn't figured out how to solve it in an original way often turns to cliché endings.

Of all the awful, unpublishable short stories ever written (and I've written several of them) probably 20 percent have something in common. The events of the story aren't really happening. It's all a dream. But the victimized reader doesn't learn that until the end of the story, and it's too late for him to change his mind about reading it. So if you've got a short story that ends with the revelation that "it was all a dream," I want you to take a match to that story immediately.

The dream ending is just one of the overused plot devices which brand the writer's manuscript as the work of an amateur. Another example is the writer's last-page announcement that the narrator of the story isn't a person at all, but is really a collie or a statue in the park or a 1952 Chevy convertible. Sometimes a beginning writer avoids resolving the crisis in a story by announcing that there really wasn't any crisis; it was all just a character playing a prank, or he settles a problem by creating an incredible coincidence such as having the two separated lovers on ships that collide, and the lovers end up on the same life raft waiting for the Coast Guard.

These devices are as common as dust mites because they solve a perplexing problem for the writer: How do I get out of this mess? The dream announcement is not an ending; it's what writers throw in when they don't have an ending. Desperation is often the thing that causes a writer to be unoriginal in his thinking. Of course the writer doesn't know he's being unoriginal. He thinks he's being terribly clever.

So, does this mean that nobody could ever write a good story that ends with a surprise narrator or a coincidence or a dream? No. "The Wizard of Oz" seems to have done well. But anything that seems to solve a major story problem so easily is rarely clever or original. It has probably been used as often as "My dog ate my homework."

The ending of a story should emerge from the nature of the story, the dynamics of the characters and the plot. An ending is not just a headline that you shout at the end to explain what happened. ("Extra, extra, read all about it, Bernice was only dreaming, she wasn't really being attacked by crazed poodles from outer space.") A story ending is a point you have been moving toward. An ending, even when it is similar to other endings, should seem to be unique to the story at hand. It should not look like an ending that could be tacked on to a hundred other stories. Like everything you write, it should be both good and original.

Credibility

Credibility is believability, and everything you write, fiction or nonfiction, must have that quality. As a writer you are probably drawn to write about the unusual, the unlikely, the strange and fascinating. These are the things which are hardest to believe. They create reader resistance. "Nah," the reader thinks, "that can't be true. You're making it up." In the case of fiction, he knows on one level that you are making it up, but successful fiction makes the reader give up that knowledge and believe every word. We'll talk more about credibility in fiction soon, but first I want to discuss credibility in nonfiction. In nonfiction you might think that just telling the truth is enough. But it's not. The truth is not automatically credible. You have to make the reader believe it.

Show That It's True

Eighty percent of the nonfiction manuscripts I've read have credibility problems. That is, the writer says that certain things are true, but he doesn't "prove" it; he doesn't show that they are true.

Here's the kind of writing I see often:

When brothers or sisters form a business partnership the fact that they are siblings compounds the tensions generated in getting a business off the ground and making decisions crucial to its own survival.

In one sense, siblings have a better chance to make it as partners than people who didn't grow up together. Strangers don't have the history which could make them stick together with the partnership when faced with serious disputes.

But in terms of power struggles siblings are more likely to carry family roles into the workplace and with them, old resentments.

The problem with that writing is that it has no credibility. The writer is saying a lot of things, but the reader has no reason to believe they are true. Credibility has got to be brought to the material.

In other sections of this book I have shown you how some writer did things the wrong way, and what I advised. This time I want to show you how a writer did it the right way. I have edited the above passage out of an article sent to me by Phyllis Feurstein of Olympia Fields, Ill. Phyllis didn't write it that way. Her article, called, "My Brother/My Business Partner," didn't have any credibility problems. Let's see why.

Two brothers who had never been able to share a bicycle go into business together. Each is so bent on getting his way, the boat-parts company nearly runs aground. A solution they settle on is: build a wall dividing the business into two parts. Each becomes chief honcho of a division and needs permission to enter the other's turf. The arrangement tempers what psychologists call "The ancient survival game of sibs."

Here Phyllis has done two things to boost credibility. She has given us an anecdote, which "shows" us the problem, instead of telling us about it. And she has alluded to psychologists, thus associating her subject with a respected, and familiar, field of inquiry.

If this sounds like a pilot for yet another TV soap based on brothers fighting for control of a company, well . . . it isn't. Off screen brothers write their own scripts and, according to partners, business consultants, and specialists in human development, they look for ways to keep their enterprises from sinking and their sibling ties afloat.

At the bottom line, the sib-run business exists for the same reason as does any other company, to produce goods and services at a profit. But being brothers compounds the tension generated in getting a business off the ground, and making decisions crucial to its own survival.

Here Phyllis is making statements about sibs who are partners, but she's also cueing the reader that these statements are coming from credible sources: partners, business consultants, and specialists in human development.

"A sib partnership is more complicated," says Peter Davids, director of the Wharton School Applied Research Center at the University of Pennsylvania. "It requires a balance of two kinds of relationships. In the contractual, it's adult to adult, a heads-up sort of behavior. Terms are negotiated and agreed upon. In the emotional, the whole person is involved and the needs are psychological and harder to satisfy."

Here Phyllis is doing perhaps the most important thing you can do to give your nonfiction credibility. She quotes an expert. She's not presenting her opinion. She's reporting what she's found out from other people. More than any one thing, this is what makes her piece read like an article instead of an essay. In the Pace chapter I said that many new writers forget to use quotes, and that quotes are needed for a nice flow. They are just as important for credibility.

In the next paragraph Phyllis quotes another expert, a Chicago consultant to troubled partnerships, and then the next paragraph:

Sam Capsouto, one-third owner of Capsouto Freres, a popular bistro among the truck docks in New York City, puts it this way: "My brothers and I developed the kind of trust you don't develop with outsiders. We learned each other's character by playing games together as kids. Sometimes we have direct communication without talking. They sense when I need help with a rowdy customer. I know how to appeal to them to get my way and how to keep from antagonizing them."

Here Phyllis is quoting again. But note that it's just a guy who's in a partnership, not an expert. All of your quotes don't have to come from experts. The man or woman on the street has credibility, too.

A few paragraphs later Phyllis writes:

The replay took a nasty turn when Terry, against Bill's wishes, sold 51 percent of the company to an outsider to raise capital for expansion. The new major stockholder had no emotional investment in the partnership. He had put in his money strictly as a means of making a return. Upon seeing Bill as a liability, he expelled the younger brother from the firm and handed the older brother a dilemma to anguish over.

Here Phyllis is showing us the type of thing that can happen in a sibling-owned business. Credibility comes from the fact that she's giving us a specific example. Many beginning writers would write something like, "If, for example, one of the brothers sold a majority interest in the company to raise money, the new owner, not being emotionally attached to a brother, might fire him." Hypothetical situations don't have the credibility of real ones. Give specific examples to back up your general statements.

"Prove It"

When you write nonfiction you need to remain aware of the reader's doubts, and his resistance. The resistance often takes the form of an unspoken, "Prove it."

You can prove you are right with some of the things we have already talked about, an anecdote that illustrates a problem, a quote from an expert, a specific example. All of those serve as proof for general statements that you make.

Not every statement you make has to have a quote or an anecdote or an example to back it up. Many statements are self-evident. If you are writing a profile of Richard Gere, the actor, and you write, "Gere emerged as a major leading man with the release of *An Officer and a Gentleman* and *Breathless*, you don't have to drag out the box office statistics to prove it. Everybody knows it. But when you write something surprising to the reader you create resistance and it's not always enough to be correct. You have to prove it. Let's say that later in the article you write, "Gere is shy with women." That's a bit surprising and you should back it up with something, such as a quote:

Actress Nushka Resnikoff, a frequent Gere companion, says, "Richard is like a timid schoolboy. We went on five dates before he even tried to kiss me, and even then he asked me first if it was okay."

"Not Me" and "That's Me"

Readers also resist by saying, "Not me." This is the reader's way of doubting that the issue he's reading about involves him. As a writer you must show the reader in what way and to what extent she might be touched by the thing you are writing about. But there is a flip side to this. If the writing lacks the credibility of quotes, examples, etc., the reader might be led to an inaccurate, "That's me." In both cases you must give the reader credible information with which to prove or disprove her assumptions. Of course none of this would apply to a profile of Richard Gere, but it would apply to articles on everything from air pollution to zinc supplements.

This next example is the lead from my article, "Wine and Sleep," which was published in *Dynamic Living,* a magazine for people over forty. In the first paragraph I cue the probable readers (over forty) that this material is relevant to them and to what degree. In the second and third paragraphs I provide the credible information and quotes to shoot down their "Not Me's." And in the fourth paragraph I knock out the inaccurate "That's Me's" by indicating which people (younger people) should not be concerned with the information at hand.

If you're forty years old a glass of wine before bed might help you sleep better. If you're fifty the wine might help even more. And if you're sixty the glass of wine might make the difference between thrashing around under the sheets all night and sleeping like the proverbial log.

Why? Well, there's a lot of reasons, but the biggest one is a mysterious substance called GABA, which is an acronym for Gamma-Amino-Butiric-Acid. GABA is found in wine, and it's also found in sleeping people, produced by the nervous system as sleep approaches. Human beings have a reduced ability to sleep well as they grow older, and a cutback in GABA production might be the reason.

"Of course, good sleep is somewhat subjective," says Dr. Robert Kastenbaum, a pioneer in the wine-sleep field, who is Superintendent of the Cushing Hospital in Framingham, Massachusetts. Cushing is a general hospital for the elderly and an extended care facility. It was there that early wine-sleep research was done in the 1960's.

"If we use the sleep of a young adult as the ideal," says Dr. Kastenbaum, "then we can say that people have more difficulty in sleeping as they grow older. They wake up more often, they sleep less overall, and they spend less time in the 'Delta Phase' which is the most restful sleep."

"What About?"

A third kind of credibility problem emerges when the reader says, "What about . . . ?"

"What about?" occurs when you have written something that contradicts something the reader believes, and you can only gain your credibility by acknowledging it, explaining it, or disproving it.

For example, if you are writing about small economy cars and how they can save the reader a fortune during an oil shortage, you have to deal with the reader's "What about the fact that the oil shortage is over?" You need to show the reader that gasoline prices could double in a matter of months, that an oil crisis could occur at any time.

This is one of the reasons why the nonfiction writer must read a variety of newspapers and magazines and just generally keep up with what's going on in the world. If you are not as well informed as your readers, you will not know their "What abouts?" and your articles will lack credibility.

Plants

A "plant" is an idea you put in the reader's mind to gain credibility for something that comes up later. Plants are used in nonfiction and fiction but they are not crucial in nonfiction.

Let's say you are writing a profile of race car driver Sturge Thibedeau and at one point you write, "After winning the Elgin 400, Thibedeau reached his wife in the grandstand by executing a series of seventeen perfect cartwheels." While this is surprising material to the reader, you don't have to go back and plant it. You can acquire instant credibility by following it with, "Thibedeau was a gymnastics champion in college, and was a member of the 1984 U.S. Olympic gymnastics team. He still works out three hours a day in the gym, as part of his training for racing."

The reader will accept that easily because it's true. The credibility was planted years ago when Thibedeau was in college. You, the writer, didn't mention it before because it was not relevant.

With fiction you could never get away with that. If you've created a character and never mentioned anything about an unusual ability, such as gymnastics expertise, and then you have him suddenly execute seventeen consecutive perfect cartwheels, you have a serious credibility problem. What the reader hears you saying is, "Oh, by the way, I forgot to tell you, but Sturge is a gymnastics champion." The reader feels previously entitled to that information, and so he gets an ugly suspicion that you are just making up history to suit a present need. At some point earlier in the story when you don't appear to need it, make a reference to your character's gymnastic prowess. Then when he does his cartwheels, there will be plenty of credibility. Here are three more examples:

1. In chapter five the luxury liner sinks. Go back to chapter one and plant some disturbing engine sounds, or some talk about the danger of icebergs on the voyage.

2. In scene twenty the hero has his gun taken away from him, but he pulls a Derringer out from under his hat and shoots the bad guys. Go back and show him putting the Derringer under his hat or tell us that he always carries a Derringer under this hat.

3. On page twenty Gail scores ten long set shots in a row. Go back to page three and show Gail practicing her long set shots.

One of the common mistakes that writers make is putting in a premonition instead of a believable plant. Instead of putting in disturbing engine sounds or iceberg warnings, the writer writes something like this: "As Jeffrey boarded the ship he had a sense of foreboding. Something didn't feel right about this voyage. For a moment he thought of leaving the ship, but he knew that would make him look foolish to his friends. So he pushed the troubling thoughts from his mind and headed for the bar."

Usually there is no explanation of why Jeffrey would have a premonition. This is not an effective plant because it doesn't add credibility. It subtracts it. The idea of somebody having a premonition about a ship sinking is less believable than just having the ship sink. The exception to that would be a story in which Jeffrey has been established as a character who has premonitions which do come true. Don't put premonitions in your stories unless you are prepared to explain them and use them to move your plot.

Keep in mind that a plant cannot just be arbitrarily dropped in anywhere to provide credibility for something that will occur later. The planted information must merge smoothly with the story. It must be doing some work besides being a plant. Otherwise it will stand out like a big red sign that says, "Hi, I'm a plant. See ya later."

Here's an example of a plant from *Dear So and So,* the novel I'm working on.

Dear So and So is the story of a man who enters a contest to replace a famous advice columnist. At the end of the book, it turns out that the contest was fixed. But if I never suggested that possibility earlier in the book, the fixed contest ending would look like a contrivance I had used to solve some of my plot problems. It would lack credibility. So, in order to create credibility for that ending, I must plant the idea that the contest could be fixed. But I must make my planted information do some other work. The successful plant contains information that could comfortably fit into the story even if it were not doing the work of a plant.

In the first chapter my character, Scotty, calls an editor, Al Jacobs, and tries to sell him an article about the contest.

> I must have sounded like a lunatic. I really was excited about the story, and I was shouting to be heard over the sound of afternoon traffic on Route 70.
>
> "It's in the bag," Al said.
>
> "Huh?"
>
> "It's in the bag."
>
> "What bag? What are you talking about?"
>
> "The bag, for Christ's sake. The contest is fixed."
>
> "How do you know?"

"Instinct," Al said. "These things are always fixed. They already know who they want."

"You're just cynical," I said, which struck me as ironic, considering my own current view of life. The pot calling the kettle cynical. "Of course it's not fixed. They wouldn't dare."

In addition to being a plant for the eventual fix, this passage is doing two other jobs. It is characterizing Al Jacobs as hard-nosed and cynical, and it is creating a reason for his turning down Scotty's story, which helps me move Scotty closer to the point of entering the contest.

Credible Characters

A character has credibility if the reader believes that the character could do, and would do, what you say she does. The character lacks credibility when the reader says, "Oh she couldn't do that," or "She wouldn't do that."

I talked to my friend Chris Keane about this. Keane is a screenwriter, a novelist, and a writing teacher.

Like all writing teachers Chris sees a lot of manuscripts in which the characters and the writer seem to have, at best, a passing acquaintance.

"Too many writers just don't know their characters," he said, "and so they have characters acting in ways that are incredible to the reader."

"For example?" I said.

"Well, one guy gave me a story in which his heroine, Lana, is a somewhat mousey young lady, meek, mild-mannered, sweet. In one scene she's walking home from the theatre and she is assaulted. She was in danger. How did she get out of the situation? Simple. She unleashed a series of vicious karate chops and sent the assailant to the hospital. The writer thought this was a pretty good scene, a lot of flying limbs, and the like."

"But?"

"But it was totally without credibility. There were two credibility problems that had to be solved. One was, *could* the character do this? All of a sudden Lana knows karate. There was never a hint of it before. So I told the writer to go back and plant some karate training, and also show us Lana's motivation for taking the training in the first place. It doesn't do us any good to plant the training if we still believe that Lana would never go to karate school.

"But there was a much more serious credibility problem with the scene. Lana was merciless in her attack. Yet she had been portrayed as meek, mild-mannered, and so forth, the kind of girl who would probably strike one blow and then run off into the night. Even if we believed she could do it, because of her training, we still didn't believe she *would* do it, because of her character as we had learned it. The girl doing the karate was just not Lana, but somebody that the writer needed at the moment. This is not a credibility problem you can solve simply by going back and planting something. The problem is that the writer didn't know his character well enough."

I asked Chris for a solution to the problem.

"Simple," he said. "Before you write a word, sit down and write a three- to five-page biography for every significant character. That's what I do. It is essential for the writer to know where his character was born, what his goals are, what his fears are, how does he feel about his mother, his father, and so forth. This may seem like a lot of extra work, but it's necessary and it actually saves a lot of time. If you do the biography you will never get writer's block. You will create real flesh-and-blood characters and you will know who they are, what they are capable of, and how they would react in any given situation."

There is one more point I want to make about credible characters, because it concerns a mistake I made often (even after I was getting published) and which I see in most of the manuscripts I read.

It is very important that your characters have a life beyond the confines of the story. Too many characters come across as actors who were hired to play a role. They seem to have no history, no future, and nothing on their minds except the business of the story. These characters lack credibility. You must create characters who seem to have a full life, who seem to go places and do things even when we are not reading about them. You can do this with a few well-placed details. When your character goes to a movie, maybe "it reminded him of a movie he had seen two years ago when he and Janet were going steady." If he pulls a jack-knife out of his pocket, maybe "it was a gift from his cousin." These details say that your character was alive two years ago and going to movies, that he had girlfriends, that he has a cousin and family, and they probably have family gatherings with cakes and balloons and everything, all of which has nothing to do with your story, but a lot to do with your character.

Incidentally, if you take Chris Keane's suggestion and write the three- to five-page biography, you will have a deep well of material from which to draw these details.

Credibility of Plot

It would take an entire book to say everything that could be said about credibility of plot. But there are a few points I want to make here and they, combined with your other reading and your own writing experience, should deepen your understanding of credibility of plot. As we go along it might seem at times that I am still talking about credibility of character instead of plot. That's the point. Credible plots emerge from credible characters.

First let's talk about Crosby Holden. Crosby lives in Dallas, Texas, and his manuscripts were the best ones I got. One was *The Great Chili Cookoff Caper,* a novel.

"Dear Crosby," I wrote, "You have a good workable story. It's orderly, it's logical, it is not confusing. You have believable characters, an exciting background, and good local color. Reading the book made me hungry for Mexican food, and that's always a good sign. But there are some problems."

Of course there were some problems. That's why he sent me the book. Incidentally, keep in mind that it is not just beginning or pre-published writers who need their books looked at. All writers do. My friend Chris Keane has published eight books, but a copy of his latest manuscript is sitting on my desk right now, awaiting my comments. When Chris finishes a manuscript he sends copies to several writer friends for their critiques and then he does another rewrite.

But anyhow, getting back to Crosby. There were a few things in his book that can help us discuss credibility of plot.

The Great Chili Cookoff Caper is a story about two boys, Kevin and Juan Pablo, who get involved with bank robbers during the festive chili cookoff weekend in a small Southwestern town.

As I've said, plot emerges from character. So it is important for characters to have strong, believable motivations in order for those motivations to fuel the forward movement of the story. Putting it another way, readers can't care that much unless they believe that the character cares that much. As Crosby's story went along, we saw that Kevin, the main character, wanted to solve the bank robbery, but we didn't really see why.

I wrote to Crosby, "As you get back into the book I think you have to give a lot more thought to motivation. What is it that keeps Kevin going? As it is, he often talks about being a hero, but that doesn't seem strong enough by itself. After all, he is putting his life in danger. Why does he want to be a hero? Is he trying to make up for some bad behavior? Does he desperately need to impress somebody? Is he trying to prove to himself that he's brave, smart, whatever? Think about this. Right now there's nothing at stake. If Kevin fails to figure out who robbed the bank and bring them to justice, it doesn't matter; he suffers no great consequence. And if he figures it out, there's no great gain. Solving it and not solving it have just about the same emotional result, and so the reader takes just a passing interest. Make the whole thing urgent. Make Kevin passionate about his need to solve this, so that we can care more. Make us really worry."

Here are some possible motivations that come to mind: 1. Kevin made a fool of himself once before on something like this. 2. Kevin acted like a coward recently and needs to redeem himself. 3. Someone Kevin cares about was victimized by the robbery.

So, credible plots emerge from credible characters having credible motivations. Can you think of three more reasons why Kevin might want to solve a bank robbery?

When you think about character motivation, think about it in a very broad way. When I wrote *Finder* about Marilyn Greene, I had index cards taped to my typewriter. On one I had written, "What does Marilyn want?" Another said, "What is Marilyn feeling?" All through the writing of the book I was reminded to think about those things. These questions are not just important for overall motivation as it affects plot. They determine how a character acts in every scene. Be like an actor. Get into the skin of every character and ask yourself, "What is my character feeling right now? Scared, happy, nervous, lonely?" Do this for all your characters before you have them act.

Crosby's other major credibility mistake was the most damaging one that writers make in this realm.

At one point in the story Kevin is on the roof of the bank robbers' van when they drive away. Juan Pablo, Kevin's friend, witnesses this. From everything we know about Juan Pablo up to this point, it is clear that his solution to the problem would be to go to the police. But he doesn't. Juan Pablo remains rather casual about the whole thing and he tells no one.

Why?

Because if Juan Pablo went to the police, that would change all the future action of the story as the author envisioned it. He didn't have Juan Pablo go to the police because that would not have worked well for the plot of the story.

This is a fatal mistake.

I wrote to Crosby, "It is just not believable that Juan Pablo would see his friend carried off on the roof of a van driven by dangerous men, and then not tell anyone. It's a case of a character acting in an unbelievable manner simply to solve one of the author's plot problems. Characters have to act out of their own nature, not the author's needs, or the story won't work. Maybe the only way to solve this is to take Juan Pablo out of the van scene and have Kevin tell him about it later."

Write this on a piece of paper and hang it over your desk:

CREDIBLE CHARACTERS ACT OUT OF THEIR OWN NATURE, NOT THE AUTHOR'S PLOT NEEDS.

Sometimes the character who is acting in an unbelievable fashion is so minor that you can't make the necessary changes. You have to change somebody or something else.

For example, a Louisiana writer sent me a novel set in the 1800s. His main character, Calvin, is seventeen years old, a pimply, gangly, sexually inexperienced youth. One night Calvin goes to a tavern where he meets Dolly—beautiful, voluptuous, twenty-one years old . . . a hot little number. Dolly takes Calvin to her room, where, between tankards of ale, she makes mad love to him all night. As he's reeling his way home at sunrise, Calvin is assaulted by sailors, who have no trouble capturing him and impressing him into duty on a ship that is sailing for England.

In this case Calvin did act out of his own nature. Any seventeen-year-old boy in his right mind would have gone to Dolly's room, especially one like Calvin who probably doesn't get many golden opportunities. The person who didn't act out of her own nature was Dolly. Why would a gorgeous and much-experienced twenty-one-year-old woman want to spend the night with a callow, seventeen-year-old, acne-plagued lad she had never met before?

Dolly had acted out of the needs of the plot. But since she was such an incidental character it would be awkwardly out of proportion to try to build some foundation for her behavior, such as: When Dolly was sixteen her seventeen-year-old boyfriend died in a button factory accident and ever since that time she has tried to recapture the feelings of being with him by seducing every seventeen-year-old boy she can get her hands on, no matter how pimply and gawky he happens to be.

The sensible way to handle this, if the Dolly scene is necessary, would be to go back and somehow convince the reader that Calvin is attractive to older women. Reconstruct his face, or his body, or his personality; do something to make us believe a woman like Dolly would get excited about Calvin and invite him to her room ten minutes after meeting him.

Here I've given you specific examples of laying a foundation, but keep in mind that almost every scene you write is a foundation for something to come later. The last page in a story or novel should seem to emerge naturally from all that has gone before. Let me give you an example of how foundation was built along the way in *Popcorn*.

Popcorn, which my wife Gail and I wrote, is about Markie Newman, twelve years old. Markie has a musical trio called Popcorn, and his goal is to make a hit record. Gail and I knew that in the last chapter of *Popcorn*, three talented twelve-year-old kids that nobody had ever heard of would play a concert in Central Park in front of 400,000 people.

We also knew that such a thing was hard to believe. So we had to lay a lot of foundation to make it credible.

1. Lance Follinsbee, a big rock star, has scheduled a free concert in Central Park. (That's not hard to believe. Everybody knows that Diana Ross and Simon and Garfunkel have done the same thing and have drawn crowds of 400,000.)

2. The father of Missy Evans, Popcorn's drummer, is a professional drummer in New York. (That's not hard to believe. If Missy is a talented musician it's not surprising that her father is.)

3. Missy's father knows Lance Follinsbee's manager, Rob Powers. (That's not hard to believe. They are both in the music industry.)

4. Missy adores Lance Follinsbee. (That's not hard to believe. She's twelve.)

5. Missy's father arranges for Popcorn to sit up front at the concert. (That's not hard to believe; he knows the manager and he loves his daughter.)

6. Markie has been trying to get publicity for Popcorn. (That's not hard to believe. He wants to make a record, he knows he needs publicity.)

7. Markie has been studying the martial arts. At one point his teacher Roger tells him to "seize the moment" of opportunity in the martial arts, and in life. At another point Roger tells Markie, "Never measure a mountain until you're on top of it." At another time Roger teaches Markie to focus his mind so that he doesn't think about his fears. Markie is very influenced by Roger. (This is not hard to believe. It's all consistent with martial arts philosophy. The fact that Markie is taking martial arts has been set up by his encounters with the bully known as Joel the Troll.)

8. Lance Follinsbee doesn't show up for the concert. (That's not hard to believe. The public has heard about stars not showing up for concerts. And, in an earlier scene, Lance is shown as nervous and insecure about facing a crowd so big.)

So all of this is woven into the plot. The kids get to the concert, they sit in front, Lance doesn't show up, and now it's time to make the reader believe that three kids could end up giving a concert in front of 400,000 people in Central Park. Markie is telling the story.

> After another minute I guess the crowd began to realize it was true—there wouldn't be any concert. There was this kind of sad feeling all around, and then a few people started to gather their things, and then a few more, and people were standing. Way off at the back of the crowd I could see that people were starting to drift away.
>
> There were a lot of people in the front rows writing in notebooks, and that's when I realized they were reporters. Then I noticed that people from the TV stations with mini-cams on their shoulders were there, too. My heart started beating faster. I turned and looked up at the stage. It looked as high as a mountain. Then I turned and looked at the reporters again. *Four hundred thousand people,* I thought. *What a way to get noticed.* I looked at the stage again. The keyboard was a lot bigger than mine but I knew I could play it. And the microphones were all set up.
>
> "This is it," I said.
>
> "This is what?" Missy said.

"The moment."

"What moment?"

"The moment Roger told me about. And if we don't seize it, it will never come again," I said, and I turned around and ran to the foot of the stairs where Rob Powers was.

"Mr. Powers, I want to go up," I said.

"Up where?"

"On stage," I said. "Popcorn. We'll play, we'll do the concert."

"But you can't do that," he said.

"Why?"

"Well . . ." he paused. "Well, there's no particular reason, I guess."

"Of course there's not," I said. "Nobody paid to get in here. Even if we're lousy they can't ask for their money back."

Mr. Powers smiled at me. "Go for it," he said. "Only, watch yourself. That stage is pretty high."

I looked up at the stage and my heart was pounding like crazy. It looked like the stage was halfway to the sky. *Just do it*, I told myself. *Don't think about it*. I wanted to close my eyes so I wouldn't see how incredibly big the crowd was, but I was afraid I'd trip. I started climbing. I counted the steps to keep my mind busy and so I wouldn't think about how afraid I could be.

Coincidence

Coincidence is the most common killer of credibility. Coincidence served Charles Dickens well, of course, but today's reader is just too sophisticated. If your plot depends on the most unlikely coincidence, your reader's suspension of belief will be shattered. She will say, "Oh come on, let's get serious. You expect me to believe *that?*"

The incredible coincidence is the hallmark of the amateur. A Vermont girl loses her puppy. The following summer her parents send her to Elgin, Illinois to spend a week with her aunt and uncle. One day she's walking home from an accordion concert. She's not fully awake yet, but she could swear that the doggy running towards her, wagging its cute little tail is . . . yes, yes, it is . . . it's Mugsie, the dog she lost in Vermont.

Well, it turns out that some people who live near her aunt had gone skiing in Vermont several months back, but they were in New York before they realized that this dog had stowed away in their car. No identification, so they kept the pooch.

It's true that such bizarre things do occur from time to time in real life, and you can read about them in the *National Enquirer,* but that doesn't make them any more believable in your fiction. The effect of a coincidence is that you failed. You didn't know how to make the story work fairly, so you dragged in an obvious and unsatisfying device.

What's particularly scandalous is that many new writers use coincidence without even getting something in return. For example, a woman in California sent me a romance novel. Elena, the main character, is a designer in a big garment factory. She has never met Todd Delaney, the owner, but she has heard he is quite dashing. By the middle of chapter one, which takes place on Monday, she is scheduled to have an interview with him on Thursday. At the end of the chapter she walks out of the building, onto a crowded street. She goes several blocks and then she trips on a curb. A man reaches out and grabs her before she can fall. He is tall, handsome, and he has hypnotic green eyes. She thanks him, and they part.

Well you won't be surprised to know that when Thursday comes around and Elena goes to Todd Delaney's office for the interview, he too is tall, handsome, and has hypnotic green eyes. *It's the same man.*

Maybe this coincidence would be acceptable if there were some point to it, if the writer were getting something in return. But she's not. Elena was already scheduled to meet Todd on Thursday and the rest of the romance emerges from that first meeting. The coincidence created reader resistance, without giving something in return. It was pointless. But hundreds of writers do this. If you are one of them, stop it. The worst kind of coincidence is one that doesn't even work for a living.

This is not to say you can never use coincidence in your stories. You can. If you are crafty, you can make the reader believe anything. The trick is to make the coincidence seem to have some logic to it.

For example, a woman sent me a short story. In this story, Merrie, the heroine, goes to a large social gathering one night at a mansion in San Francisco. She walks out into the garden for a little air and is assaulted by a man who tries to rape her. About a year later Merrie is in Boston, checking into the Copley Square Hotel, and guess who's behind her in line? The man who tried to rape her in San Francisco.

Hmmm.

The problem here is that we've gone from San Francisco to Boston, so we are dealing with the whole United States, and the two people we want to meet have to be drawn from a pool of well over two hundred million people. Pretty far-fetched. The way to make this seem less coincidental is to reduce the size of the people pool they are being drawn from. In this story Merrie was a college administrator. I told the author to make the original San Francisco assault occur at a convention for college administrators. Then a year later, when Merrie travels to Boston for the annual convention she runs into the same guy. He's there because he's also a college administrator. Now instead of our coincidence being drawn from a pool of over two hundred million Americans, it is drawn from the much smaller pool of college administrators who go to the annual convention, and it meets all of the story's requirements.

Here's another example. Let's say there's a reindeer that none of the other reindeer like. They all make fun of him and they won't let him play any of their reindeer games. But at the end of the story you want this reindeer to be selected for the most important job of the year, leading Santa's sleigh on Christmas Eve. Seems pretty far-fetched, doesn't it, that the least popular reindeer would be selected? But you could make it believable if you could establish a logical connection between those two things. What if the reason they made fun of him was the same reason that he was selected to lead the sleigh? Maybe he has a bright and shiny red nose, and it helps them see where they are going one foggy Christmas eve? The logical connection would make the reader say, "Of course!" instead of "Incredible!"

Can you think of ways to make these coincidences believable?

1. Two men meet in a bar and go through 300 pages of adventure together. At the end it turns out that one is the other's long lost brother.

2. A boy, dreaming of treasure, finds a treasure chest in his cellar.

3. A brother and sister, separated in childhood, end up married to each other.

4. A bounty hunter, chasing an outlaw, learns that the outlaw is the man who saved his father's life years ago.

To gain credibility for coincidence number one we could put the opening scene in a bar that's in the neighborhood where the young men were born. Though the two have lost touch, maybe each goes back to the old neighborhood from time to time.

Or we could have the introduction based on something the brothers might have in common. Maybe their father was a dart champion and when he abandoned them he left behind several expensive sets of darts. When the boys were put in separate foster homes each had a set of darts. Now they meet in the bar because they are both shooting darts.

The point is to set a foundation so that when the reader finds out they are really brothers, it seems to make sense.

Subtlety

In an instructional book like this, messages must be repeated several times to be brought home. But repeating a point several times is exactly what I'm going to advise you not to do. So at the risk of not being subtle in the telling, I must tell you to be subtle in your writing.

Being subtle doesn't mean you can't say something three times or ten times. It means don't say it three times when one time is enough. Being subtle means don't shout to, or wink at, the reader to make sure he gets your meaning. Being subtle means don't tell the reader something if you are also showing it to him. And being subtle means don't tell or show the reader anything you don't have to.

Don't Overstate

In most of the manuscripts I read, the writer writes the same thing too many times in different ways. This is known as hitting the reader over the head with a sledge hammer and, not surprisingly, readers don't much care for it. When a writer does this I point it out by underlining the phrases or sentences that are repeating information. Here is an example

from a manuscript I have read:
Compare

Lately Ben had been *acting spacey*. Since the last day of school he had been *acting really weird*. He'd been sleeping all day and *doing bizarre things* at night.

with

Since the last day of school Ben had been sleeping all day and doing bizarre things at night.

You must avoid overstatement, not just within sentences but throughout the manuscript. I'll give you an example from *Finder*'s fourth chapter, which I have just rewritten.

Early in the chapter, I wanted to show that Marilyn Greene was interested in finding missing persons, even when she was a kid. In the original chapter I told a three-hundred-word story about a little girl disappearing from Marilyn's neighborhood, and how fascinated Marilyn was with the case. Then I told another story about a missing boy whose case Marilyn followed in the newspapers. And then I told a story about Marilyn, as a teenager, finding a lost little boy asleep on a bread counter at a grocery store, and how good Marilyn felt about being the one to find him.

Each story was interesting, but all three were there for the same reason, to show Marilyn's childhood interest in missing persons. When I rewrote the chapter I cut out two of the stories. The reader didn't need three stories to get the point. I showed him one, and he could imagine the rest.

This does not mean you should never use two or three anecdotes or examples to make a point. It all depends on the material at hand and the reader's knowledge. In this book, for example, I sometimes feel that I need three examples to be sure I've gotten my point across. Other times I'm certain that one example is enough. In the *Finder* chapter, I wasn't presenting new and complex information. I used an anecdote to make a general point about Marilyn. Two more anecdotes making the same point were just slowing the book down, so I got rid of them. (However, if the additional anecdotes had been so compelling that by themselves they were exciting storytelling, I would have used them. I will sacrifice subtlety if I feel that I am giving the reader a great yarn, a juicy bit of gossip, or a truly fascinating bit of relevant information in return.)

Overstatement occurs when the writer is uncertain about whether or not she has communicated her meaning. She tries to hammer it home with a few more words. She writes "He laughed happily," because she is not sure that "He laughed" will show the happiness. She writes "Leslie was terribly frightened and her heart pounded" because she doesn't trust the reader to see the fright in "Her heart pounded." Instead of compressing her meaning, she dilutes it.

Being subtle means having faith in the reader.

The reader will get your meaning more easily than you think, and it takes only a few well-chosen words to get your thoughts across.

Don't Shout or Wink

One common mistake that beginning writers make is calling attention to their writing with some visual cue such as exclamation points, unnecessary quotation marks, upper case letters, or italics. Don't call attention to the fact that something you just wrote is supposed to be sarcastic, funny, or whatever. If you try to cue your reader that something is supposed to be funny, for example, your cue becomes the literary equivalent of canned laughter on TV situation comedies, or those moronic cavalry charges that are played at basketball games to tell fans when they should be excited. If the reader thinks something is funny, he will laugh. If he doesn't think it's funny, you're not helping yourself by telling him that it was supposed to be.

Don't Tell If You Are Showing

In the style books you have read and in the style section of this book you have heard the advice, "Show, don't tell." Of course you can't show everything. Showing often takes more words than you can afford to spend. But when you do show something, it is often best to let the reader discover it for himself. Be subtle. Don't tell the reader what you have shown him or what you are about to show him, if the "showing" can stand on its own.

Here is an example from a student's manuscript:
Compare

By ten o'clock my *super-organized husband*—who *never forgets anything*—has everything packed and loaded. He's put gas in the car, pillows in the back seat, and cash in my pocketbook. He *is the efficient one in the family.*

with

By ten o'clock my husband has put gas in the car, pillows in the back seat, and cash in my pocketbook.

With the words I have italicized, the writer is telling us what the action of the sentence is showing us. But the reading experience is more pleasant for the reader who discovers for himself what an efficient guy the writer's husband is.

Keep in mind that showing can't always stand on its own. Often you have to show and tell, or tell and show. In nonfiction you will often tell the reader something, and then show him the same thing with an example. An example usually doesn't make any sense unless the reader has first been told what it is an example of.

The style rule "Show, don't tell," is also a rule about subtlety, and it goes much deeper than the sentence level. Here is a larger example, also from Chapter Four of *Finder*.

In one scene I had Marilyn, age eighteen, applying for a job as a state trooper. I began by telling the reader that Marilyn really wanted the job badly, that it meant the world to her. I wrote, "It sounds now like an advertisement on the back of a matchbook cover, but at the time it was the most important thing in the world to me."

In the rewrite I eliminated that "telling" sentence because I knew the reader would discover it for himself in the scene that followed:

"Let me tell you something, young lady," McNamara said. "There has never been a woman state trooper in New York and there never will be. It's not a woman's job. Now you should go home and forget about this nonsense."

I was shocked. He could not have hurt me more if he had yanked a bullwhip out of his desk drawer and lashed me with it. With a single thoughtless statement he had gutted my dream. I was numb.

As we turned the corridor I cringed under the touch of his hand which caressed my shoulder. I stared intently at the beige wall across from his door and I bit tightly into my lip. I did not want to cry, not in front of this man.

By showing Marilyn's reaction to the rejection, I have led the reader to the conclusion, "That job was important to Marilyn." Anytime you can lead a reader to a conclusion instead of telling him your conclusions, your writing will work better. Being subtle means letting the reader make his own discoveries. *Finder,* of course, is nonfiction, but because it is narrative nonfiction, you can easily see that the point applies as much to fiction.

Let the Reader Participate

Being subtle in your stories and articles means much more than just avoiding overstatement. And "showing" often means letting the reader look into his own life experience. Subtlety is at the heart of the relationship between the writer and the reader. The extent to which you are subtle is the extent to which you allow the reader to collaborate on your story, to fill in the blanks.

To use an obvious example, you would never write in a medical article, "After the injections small amounts of red blood remain on the tip of the needle," because you know that the reader knows the blood is red. The reader imagines the red without your help, just as he imagines the fright when you tell him that Leslie's heart was pounding.

The reader knows a good deal more than the color of blood. In fact, his store of knowledge is the most important element in your manuscript. Make him use it. Your reader lives in the same world you live in and because of that you can make some assumptions about what he does and does not know.

Take, for example, this opening from Erich Segal's *The Class:*

My Harvard twenty-fifth reunion is next month and I am scared to death.

Scared to face all my successful classmates, walking back on paths of glory, while I have nothing to show for my life except a few gray hairs.

Today a heavy red-bound book arrived that chronicles all the achievements of The Class of '58. It really brought home my own sense of failure.

I stayed up half the night just staring at the faces of the guys who once were undergraduates with me, and now are senators and governors, world-famous scientists and pioneering doctors. Who knows which of them will end up on a podium in Stockholm? Or the White House lawn?

And what's amazing is that some are still married to their first wives.

Here Segal is making a lot of assumptions about the reader's knowledge. He's assuming that the reader knows that the Nobel Prizes are given in Stockholm, that the President of the United States lives in the White House, etc. But I particularly want you to focus on that last sentence.

And what's amazing is that some are still married to their first wives.

Only thirteen words, but because Segal knows that the reader lives in the same divorce-riddled culture as he does, the sentence speaks volumes. It suggests the price of success that has been paid by many of the graduates along those "paths of glory." It says that most of the graduates have been through divorces. It also tells us that the narrator has probably seen many divorces among his friends. Otherwise, he wouldn't find it *amazing*.

The sentence describes a whole dimension in the lives of the narrator and his subjects, and it is based entirely on the author's faith that the reader knows that divorce is epidemic in America.

If Segal had written something less subtle, like, "And with the incredible growth in the divorce rate since 1958, it's amazing that some of them are still married to their first wives," the sentence would not have had the same effect. By letting the reader bring his knowledge of divorce into the story, Segal has allowed the reader to par ticipate in the creation of the story.

Subtlety in Dialogue

Subtlety, as I've said, is often forsaken when the writer loses faith in the reader's ability to figure out what's going on. In dialogue, the writer who is afraid that the reader won't know who is being spoken to often resorts to direct address. It's awkward, it's artificial, and it marks the writer as an amateur. Here's an example from one of the manuscripts I read:

> "Look, Cal, the man is lying on the porch with a gun in his hand. Of course it was suicide."
>
> "Captain Frey, I don't think so."
>
> "I'm telling you, Cal, the guy knocked himself off."

"I don't believe it for a second, Captain Frey. It's too much of a co-incidence."

Can you hear the awkwardness, the intrusive quality of the direct references? The dialogue is like a stream and the "Cal"'s and "Captain Frey"'s are like boulders interrupting the flow. There's no subtlety. Now read the dialogue without the "Cal"'s and "Captain Frey"'s and you'll hear the dialogue flow smoothly.

The use of direct address is just a bad habit, and you can break it easily. If you glance at a page and see that you have one character using the other's name ten times, cross out at least eight of them. Then read the dialogue. You'll see that you didn't need them.

If you are making this mistake because you think the reader won't know who is speaking to whom, don't worry about it. The reader has a number of clues. The change in paragraphs signals a new speaker. The attribution (he said, she said, etc.) shows who is speaking. The style of speech often tells the reader who is speaking. And, of course, the content of the dialogue tells the reader who is speaking. If we know that Annette is the bank teller, then, when Barney says, "Fill this bag with twenty dollar bills or I'll blow your head off," there's no doubt about who is the speaker and who is the listener.

The only time you should use the direct address is when you are getting something in return for it, such as characterization or story value. The word "Mickey" in "Well, Mickey, I hear you've got a new job," doesn't do any work. But if you wrote, "Well, honey, I hear you've got a new job," or "Well, jerko, I hear you've got a new job," then the direct address is telling the reader how the speaker feels about the person she is speaking to, and it communicates the tone of the conversation.

Avoid Heavy-Handed Dialogue

Heavy-handed dialogue occurs when the reader can see the writer at work, loading the dialogue with a lot of information that just wouldn't come out in normal conversation. Most of the manuscripts I read are loaded with heavy-handed dialogue. Here's an example:

"You and I stole ten thousand dollars, Sam. We embezzled it from the Valentine Corporation, and when Jervis inspects the books on June fifth he's going to know it. Your brother Warren is a lawyer and he's married to Valentine's sister. I say we tell him," Tony said.

"We can't tell anybody. You're already on probation for beating up that guy at the Rainbow Lounge last summer, and how long do you think I would last as a cashier at Rockingham Race Track if they knew I stole ten thousand bucks on my last job?"

The dialogue is the opposite of subtle because each speaker is contributing information that the listener already has, and the reader knows it. It's obvious that the dialogue is there not to inform the characters, but because the writer wants to communicate it to the reader. To get an idea of how silly heavy-handed dialogue sounds, just imagine a wife kissing her husband goodbye in the morning and saying, "So long, dear. Have a good day at the Prudential Insurance Company."

Subtle dialogue is lean and to the point. It should not be bloated with details and background information.

There are two ways to solve the heavy-handed dialogue problem. One is to be direct, not devious. For example:

Sam's brother was a lawyer and he was married to Valentine's sister.

"We've got to tell your brother," Tony said. "He's the only one who can help us."

This is not disturbing to the reader because it implies what Tony was thinking. The reader will believe that Tony was thinking about the fact that Sam's brother is a lawyer who is married to Valentine's sister. The reader won't believe that Tony would announce that information to Sam, who obviously knows.

The other way to repair this heavy-handed dialogue is to be devious, but not direct. You can get information across to readers in dialogue smoothly if you can make the reader believe the character would say that.

A speaker can believably repeat information known to the listener if the information answers a question, or requires emphasis. For example:

"Ten thousand bucks, Sam, that's what we stole, and I don't think the Valentine Corporation is going to overlook it when they find out."

"How are they going to find out?"

"Jervis is checking the books on June 1st. He'll spot it. We've got to tell your brother."

"What the hell has my brother got to do with this?"

"He's a lawyer, isn't he? He's married to Valentine's sister. He can get us off the hook."

"No. We can't tell anybody."

"Why not?"

"You're already on probation for that fiasco at the Rainbow Lounge."

"Look, I never beat that guy up. I was framed."

"Doesn't matter. The court says you did it. And what about me? You think the Rockingham Race Track is going to be thrilled to find out one of their cashiers stole ten thousand dollars from his last employer?"

How can you spot heavy-handed dialogue in your own writing? Well, keep in mind that if a speaker is giving a listener information that the listener doesn't *need*, then the speaker should be serving some need of his own. If the reader is the only person who's getting anything out of it, then the dialogue is heavy-handed.

Putting It All Together

Now let's see how a skillful writer might take all of these points about subtlety and apply them to his work. My example is fiction, but it could just as well be nonfiction.

Jim Bellarosa's short story, "A Horse of a Different Color," serves as a good example of subtlety. The story, published in *The New England Sampler,* was nominated for the Pushcart Prize, which is given annually to the best stories published in the smaller magazines.

In the story, the narrator is a farmer named Jody. Jody tells about another farmer, Forest Logg, who steals whatever he can. Forest's main character trait, the fact that he is a thief, is subtly, but clearly, noted in the second paragraph.

A neighbor was a fool to leave anything he valued lying in the open, because if Forest came by on a scouting cruise the object usually vanished that night. Next day, as a soft breeze combed through his sparse white hair, Forest could look you dead in the eye, and in the gentlest tone quickly fabricate the most outlandish but logical legend to account for his possession of another's property. And then in the same calm voice he'd declare God a genius for inventing the Seventh Commandment.

Bellarosa's story is charming, and it works perfectly because he also tells his outlandish tale "in the gentlest tone." It is subtle. The writer never breaks the spell of humor by calling your attention to the fact that it is supposed to be humorous. He doesn't wink at the reader.

For example, soon after Jody inherited the farm, he found a note about Forest, left by Jody's dead uncle. Instead of having the uncle overstate Forest's inclination to steal, Bellarosa has the uncle's note read:

> If neighbor Logg at the foot of the hill should outlive me, I urge you to secure every object you add to your new estate. Unless you do, you may find a rapid erosion of your ownership. Good luck, Jody.

Here, Bellarosa is also doing what Erich Segal did in the earlier example. He is allowing the reader to bring his imagination into the story. Instead of describing or characterizing the long relationship between Forest Logg and Jody's uncle, Bellarosa has written two sentences that make us imagine all the thefts and recoveries over the years.

Three weeks later, a bag of fertilizer is stolen during the night. In the morning, Jody walks down to Logg's farm and while the two men are talking in the yard, Orrin Growler, a neighbor, drives up. Instead of telling us again the well-established fact that Forest Logg is a crafty old thief, Bellarosa shows us by writing simply:

> Orrin had lost a scythe a few days earlier and had come to take it back home.

There is an implication, rather than an announcement, that if anything in the county is missing, Forest Logg probably has it.

Jody buys a chestnut-colored horse that has one ear missing. The next day the entire horse is missing. Of course, Jody goes to visit Forest. While the two men are talking, Forest Logg's new horse comes out of the barn and stands between them. Forest's horse also has one ear, but the horse is black.

In the dialogue that follows, many less experienced writers would have been tempted to overstate, to wave their hands for applause, by writing like this:

"I didn't know you had a horse," I needled. Without a second's pause, Forest spoke. "I have a black horse. This is it," he replied shamelessly.

"Oh really! I don't suppose you noticed that he only had one ear when you bought him," I said, knifing him with my sarcasm. His lies had gotten me angry.

Instead of throwing in extra words that drain the humor from the scene, Bellarosa used simple, understated dialogue and little else to make the scene work. He wrote:

I said, "I cannot see you, Forest. Something has come between us. Do you see it?"

Forest called over, "Yes. It is a horse."

"I didn't know you had a horse."

"I have a black horse. This is it."

"Did you know he only had one ear when you bought him?"

"Yes."

An odor drifted to my nostrils.

"Forest," I called, "I smell black paint."

"I painted my roof."

"You were sensible to paint something that was dead."

"I learned to do so from my father."

"Why did you merely buy a one-eared horse?"

"Because noises don't distract them half so easy when they are working."

"I bought the one-eared type because they are cheaper," I shouted.

"We both had good reasons."

"I would like to have a horse just like this one between us," I said, "a one-eared black type."

"You have good taste in horses."

Tension

I've been mentally flipping coins to decide whether to call this chapter "Tension" or "Suspense." Since my paperback dictionary says that one definition of tension is "uneasy suspense" I've decided to go with tension. However, as we proceed, please keep that word "suspense" in mind.

Tension is not just something that you put into your dramatic last scene when the ax murderer is hiding in the closet. It is a cord, or a series of cords, that stretch across every paragraph that you write. And tension is not always a matter of life or death. "Will he kiss her?" is tension. "Will she slap his face or melt in his arms?" That is tension. Tension is a vital element in everything that you write. It is the thing that makes your reader turn pages.

Get your reader into that state of "uneasy suspense" and keep him there. That means the reader should always be uncertain about what's coming up and should always be asking questions. Tension can come from what's happening in a story, from the words and sentences you use to tell the story, and even from the fact that you're telling the story. "Why is he telling me this?" is a reader question which creates tension.

Find Tense Words

You can add tension to your story at every level, beginning with individual words.

Certain words have a sense of urgency or danger about them, and as you go back through your manuscripts you should look for opportunities to insert words that create tension.

In this scene from *Finder* I have italicized a few of the words which I think create tension that would not be present in some of their synonyms.

> We reached the woods at the end of the yard. I kept moving forward, stepping onto a path of beaten down grass that worked its way between the trees. Billy turned left *abruptly* before we could enter the woods. I felt his hand tugging *urgently* at my elbow.
>
> "We went this way," he said.
>
> I knew I was walking with a murderer.
>
> I knew this had been the last walk Mark Feldman had ever taken. I knew that Billy didn't want to take me to the place where he had murdered his best friend.
>
> I moved slowly along beside Billy, not frightened, but *cautious*. I didn't want to push the button that could make Billy feel *threatened*.

As you probe your manuscript for opportunities to put in tense words, think particularly of:

> Words of delay, such as "paused," "waited," and "froze."
> Compare: *"I have terrible news to tell you," he said. "Scully is dead."*
>
> *"I have terrible news to tell you." He paused. "Scully is dead," he said.*
>
> Words that imply fear, such as "defended," "hid," and "fled."
> *When he heard Virgil's footsteps approach he went in the closet.*
>
> *When he heard Virgil's footsteps approach he hid in the closet.*
> Words of danger, such as "weapon," "fatal," and "pain."
> *The sensation shot all the way up his leg.*
>
> *The pain shot all the way up his leg.*

Words of urgency, such as "inevitable," "imperative," and "deadline."

Walker knew that if he didn't land this account his resignation would be necessary.

Walker knew that if he didn't land this account his resignation would be inevitable.

Arrange Sentences with Tension in Mind

Obviously the way to write tense sentences is to use tense words, such as we've just discussed. But there's more. Tension comes not just from what sentences you write, but from the order in which you write them. Tension comes from the way in which you reveal information.

Let's imagine that you have written a paragraph, and now you want to rewrite in order to put tension into it.

When Tom got back to the farmhouse Sally had moved out and he was delighted. Her key to the front door lay on the kitchen table, along with a note that said she had gone to live with Sammy. Upstairs he found her dresser drawers empty and the closet door was open.

That's a nice enough little paragraph. There's nothing terribly wrong with it, but there is no tension in it because it answers all your questions before you have a chance to ask them. In the first sentence we know what happened and how Tom feels about it. There's nothing suspenseful about the key and note on the table, since we already know she's gone. And since we know she has moved out, we never ask, "Why are her dresser drawers empty?"

The way to get tension into that paragraph is to reveal the information in the opposite order.

Tom got into the bedroom and saw that the closet door was open. (Why?) Sally's clothes were gone. (What will he do now?) He pulled open her dresser drawers. (What will this reveal?) They were empty. (How will he react?) He ran downstairs to the kitchen. (Why the kitchen?) That's where Sally always left her key when she went away on trips. (Will it be there now?) The key was on the kitchen table, along with a note. (What does it say?) The note said she had left him to live with Sammy. (How does he feel about this?) Tom smiled. He was delighted to be rid of the bitch.

You can create tension by changing the way you reveal information within individual sentences, too.

If your story is about a teenaged girl who isn't sure which twin brother has asked her to the prom, Glenn or Todd, and you wrote, "Todd was standing there when she opened the door," you can pull the tension cord a little tighter by changing it to, "When she opened the door, Todd was standing there," or you can pull the cord a lot tighter by writing, "The boy who had come to pick her up was Todd."

Milk the Tension

Sometimes you will find in your early drafts that you missed an opportunity for attention-grabbing tension, not because you put information in the wrong order, but because you gave it away too soon. Here is part of another scene from *Finder* in which I had missed a great opportunity to create reader tension.

> So I put the dog on a down-stay and I made my way gingerly across this bizarre-looking bridge in the dark. When I got to the other side I came into a clearing. I scanned the field with my flashlight and there staring back at me was a full-grown lion.

When my wife Gail read this paragraph she had a sense of dissatisfaction about it. I reread it and I could see the problem. I had told my readers there was a lion before I even gave them a chance to worry about the possibility of something dangerous lurking in the dark. I had deprived my readers of the tension. So I rewrote the material like this.

> I put Kili on a down-stay and I gingerly made my way in the dark across this bizarre-looking bridge. When I got to the other side I came to a stand of pine trees and then a clearing. There was only a fraction of a moon and the pine trees that towered over the area made the clearing darker. I stood quietly for a moment, thinking what an odd profession it was that led a lady into the Georgia woods alone at night with a dog waiting on the other side of a weird bridge. Suddenly something didn't feel right. There was a presence near me.

I thought I heard something move. I scanned the field with my flashlight. I didn't see anything. I felt afraid, but I didn't know why. Again I scanned with the light. Very slowly this time I swept my light across the darkness in a long arc. As I reached the end of the arc something flashed at me. It was a pair of eyes watching me in the dark. I turned the light back, and there, staring at me, was a full-grown lion.

A Tension Game

Here's a tension game you can play. Below are five sentences. For each one, imagine the three sentences that led up to it and write them down. The sentences you write should be like a cord that is pulled tightly until the last sentence.

1. "I want a divorce," she said.
2. The telephone line had been cut.
3. Ten thousand dollars was missing.
4. Their lips touched, oh so gently.
5. "Yes," Carlin told the crowd that night in September, "I'm the one responsible."

Here's one way to do the first:

As soon as Tom walked through the door Dottie went to the liquor cabinet. Her hand was shaking as she poured more than the usual amount. With tears in her eyes she turned and faced him. "I want a divorce," she said.

Tension in Nonfiction

Even though the two examples I gave you from *Finder* are nonfiction, that book is a narrative and the style is more suggestive of fiction. Tension is just as important in magazine profiles, biographies, interview pieces, and most other forms of nonfiction. As with fiction, tension in nonfiction comes with unanswered questions and uncertain outcomes. Here's an example:

Cleveland Amory, writing about actor George C. Scott in *Parade*, begins with a title that creates questions: "The Loves and Hates of George C. Scott." The reader keeps reading to find out what George C.

Scott loves, and is even more tantalized by the question, "What (or who) does George C. Scott hate?" Will it turn out to be a well-known celebrity? Will it be controversial?

Early in the article Amory notes that most interviewers had found Scott "either unavailable or so difficult as to make more than one wish that he had been." This creates more tension. The reader keeps reading to find out if Scott is going to be "difficult."

A few paragraphs later Amory writes, "I had assumed lunch might be involved and was pleased to note a large salad bowl of shrimp and cheese on the sideboard. Scott ignored this, however, and steered me into the den." More tension. There are later references to the shrimp and cheese bowl. That bowl is a tension creator. Why is it there, and why is Amory telling us it's there? We know that Amory is a pro and he's not calling our attention to the salad bowl for no reason. Tension is coming from "Who's going to get the shrimp and cheese?"

So while Amory etches a profile of George C. Scott through quotes and observations, he continually creates questions in our minds to keep us reading. That's what you should do. These are not questions that stay at the front of the reader's mind, but at some deep level the reader should always be asking, "What about that bowl of cheese and shrimp?" Remember that creating questions is only half the job. You have to answer them or you're going to have a reader who is still tense after he finishes your story, and he's going to blame you. He'll be annoyed with you just as you will be annoyed with me if I don't tell you what happened to George C. Scott's bowl of cheese and shrimp.

Scott fed it to his dog.

A tension-creating device is not just tacked on to an article. It can be something as provocative as a loaded pistol, or as innocuous as a bowl of cheese and shrimp, but it must be relevant. Amory was writing a profile of a man who is "difficult," a man who is widely portrayed as cranky, cantankerous, a highly talented curmudgeon. So when Scott served that huge bowl of expensive food to his dog it was a wonderful detail that revealed character. That is *why* Amory used it. The salad bowl as a tension-producer is *how* he used it. If Scott had not served the food to his dog, then Amory probably would never have mentioned the bowl.

Surface Tension

Just the fact that you've got action scenes in your story doesn't mean you've got enough tension. Bob Reiss, a novelist who has published several thrillers, tells me that when he was a teenager he wrote a novel called *Cauldron*, which has never been published. The book was about militants taking over Houston. Reiss's militants blocked the highways and sealed off the city. They held all the people as hostages, they made demands on the government, they did lots of nasty things. Reiss says there were all sorts of greedy and violent characters in his book. He sent the book off to Scott Meredith, the New York literary agent, and Reiss was surprised when it came back rejected with a letter that said, among other things, that the book lacked tension.

Reiss couldn't understand it. Here were hundreds of pages about violent people taking over a large American city. People were getting killed left and right, the U.S. army was in there, and greedy politicians were all over the place. And no tension?

"These larger issues gave the book a kind of conceptual tension," Reiss says. "What Meredith was talking about was line-by-line tension."

This is known as surface tension, and everything you write should have it. Bob Reiss gives this example of surface tension:

"The cowboys are on their way to Fort Cheyenne to reinforce the ranchers. The ranchers are stuck in Fort Cheyenne, surrounded by vicious sheepherders. The sheepherders are sick of being pushed around by the cattle ranchers.

"This is a situation with overall tension because we want to know who will win and who will live. But what about line-by-line tension? Look at the three groups. Line-by-line tension is easy for the cattle ranchers and the sheepherders. They're in the middle of a fight. The life and death issues are there all the time.

"But suppose for some reason you have to write three consecutive chapters about the cowboys, the guys coming to the rescue. The cowboys have two hundred miles to ride. The readers know nothing's going to happen until they get there. So where's the tension for the next ninety pages?

"Well, one kind of tension is in the interplay of characters, what they want, who wants to lead the group, who advises them to go the wrong way. One of them is a saboteur. One of them has love problems back in Laredo and the farther away he gets from Laredo the worse the problems get. In action books much of the tension comes not so much from action as from the *expectation* of action, or conflict. Suppose, for instance, just as the cowboys were setting off on their two-hundred mile ride we saw the local Sioux Indian chief instructing his men, 'We'll ambush those cowboys somewhere along the way.'

"Well, bingo, even if those Indians never attack, there's suddenly danger offstage all through the otherwise eventless ride. Every time the camp goes to sleep and leaves only one guard, every time a lone cowboy strolls out into the plain to brood about his girlfriend in Laredo, or write poetry about rattlesnakes, he's in danger. Every time the slow-witted and otherwise boring mess sergeant falls behind the group with his chuck wagon, we are tense, wondering if he will become the first victim."

Keep tension in mind as you tend to all the other aspects of your writing. With description, remember that a tree is a lot more interesting if there might be an Indian hiding behind it. With characterization, you could give your heroine the fear of something that might occur, such as darkness. That would create a lot more tension than the fear of something that probably won't happen, such as the fear of being hit by a falling helicopter.

Put Tension in Dialogue

In dialogue, an unfinished sentence, an unanswered question, or a cutting remark can create reader tension. But tension in dialogue is too important to be left to those occasional devices. Tension is the heart of successful dialogue, and all of your dialogue should have it.

The following dialogue is believable, but it is not exciting. It would not hold a reader's interest for long because it lacks tension.

"I'm glad you made it," Ellen said when her mother arrived at the door. "I was getting worried."

Hazel came in and dropped her bags on the floor. "I got tied up in traffic on the Connecticut Turnpike. It's a real mess today."

"Did you stop to eat?"

"Yes, I stopped at Burger King for one of those, what do you call them?"

"Whoppers," Ellen said. "They call them Whoppers."

Good dialogue creates questions in the reader's mind. It makes him wonder what will be said next. It makes the reader tense.

Tension could be added to that dialogue in several ways. You could put tension directly into the spoken words.

"Well, you finally made it," Ellen said when her mother arrived at the door. "I was getting worried. I hope you at least had enough sense to stop and eat. You know how your blood sugar is."

"I ate, I ate."

"Where, Ma, where did ya eat?"

"I stopped at Burger King. I had one of those Big Macs."

"Whoppers, Ma. Whoppers, that's what they call them. Big Macs are at McDonald's."

"Okay, so I had a Whopper."

In that example, the tension is between the characters and it comes out in the words they speak. However, tension in a dialogue scene doesn't have to be in the spoken lines. It can be between the lines.

In this next example I will leave the dialogue just as it was originally, but I will increase reader interest by adding tension between the lines of dialogue. Also, I will change the source of the tension to show you that the two characters don't have to be antagonistic toward each other.

"I'm glad you made it," Ellen said when her mother arrived at the door. "I was getting worried."

Hazel came in and dropped her bags on the floor. She stood by the counter as if she needed it to hold herself up and she struggled to take deep breaths. For the first time Ellen saw her mother as old, frail. The light had gone from her eyes. Ellen's heart pounded.

"I got tied up in traffic on the Connecticut Turnpike. It's a real mess today," Hazel said when she finally caught her breath.

"Did you stop to eat?"

"Yes, I stopped at Burger King for one of those, what do you call them?"

"Whoppers," Ellen said impatiently. "They call them Whoppers."
Tonight I'll cook, she thought. Yes, she would cook a good health-
ful meal for her mother and then everything would be all right.

So tension is that quality of "something else going on" during the
dialogue. It's what makes the reader concerned enough or curious
enough to keep reading even when the spoken words are mundane.

Now maybe you're saying, "That's great, Gary, I get the point.
But what if it's just Ma arriving for a visit, and I don't want any tension
between her and Ellen and I don't want her looking old and frail? What
if I don't want something else going on?"

If that's the case, then there's no reason to write the scene with dialogue. You'll just bore the reader. Simply write, "Ma arrived," and get
on with your story. Remember, if the reader doesn't care what happens
next, then the dialogue isn't working.

Here's a game I use at my seminars for getting tension into dialogue.

Below is an example of what good, tense dialogue might look like
without the spoken words. I'll provide you with a series of events and
feelings. You replace them with spoken words. In the future when
you're having a hard time writing dialogue, imagine it this way first, as
waves of feeling being exchanged between two people.

Anne criticizes Ray.

Ray is hurt by Anne's remark.

Anne thinks Ray is being too sensitive.

Ray thinks Anne is being too insensitive.

Anne thinks Ray is wrong.

Ray thinks Anne is wrong.

Anne thinks Ray is making a big deal out of nothing.

Ray reminds Anne about another critical remark she made last
month.

Anne thinks Ray shouldn't bring up old fights.

Ray says he's only trying to make a point about Anne's critical nature.

Anne doesn't see any point to his remark.

Ray thinks Anne always misses the point.

Anne is sure that Ray doesn't have a point.

Ray thinks Anne is refusing to admit he's right.

Anne thinks Ray is being a jerk about the whole thing.

Ray wants to slap Anne's face.

Anne feels that Ray is a wimp.

Ray wants to tell Anne off once and for all.

Anne wants to leave.

Ray threatens Anne.

Anne threatens Ray.

Pulling the Tension Cord

We have discussed tension in isolated ways, tense words, tense sentences, surface tension, etc. Now let's see what happens when an experienced writer works that quality of tension into every aspect of her writing.

A few months ago I read an excellent novel called *In Shadow* by Trish Janeshutz (Ballantine). Janeshutz is a master at choosing the right word, and that talent goes a long way toward lifting her book above similar books. She is also expert at manipulating the tension cord, which is how I visualize tension in a story. Janeshutz knows how to gradually tighten the cord, when to let it out slightly, and when to give it a yank that will scare hell out of the reader.

Here is how she begins *In Shadow:*

> He watched as she made her way through the trees toward the parking lot, her lovely head jerking at the slightest noise. She clutched her purse to her right side and her briefcase to her left, as if to draw the air around her for protection.

In the first sentence Janeshutz suggests that this woman has something to be nervous about, and that makes us nervous. In the next sentence the words "clutched" and "protection" are carefully chosen. If she had "held" her purse and tried to draw the air around her for "comfort," the tension cord would go slack.

> She knew she was being followed, he thought, and her terror thrilled him. He could imagine the adrenaline coursing wildly through her body, impelling her to look around. But she wouldn't.

In the dark, dry leaves crackling underfoot, knowing would be worse than what might only be imagined.

Janeshutz in confirming our worst fears. We suspected that something dreadful was going to happen, and after she made us worry long enough, she has come right out and said it. So now what does she do to keep the tension going?

> The walkway turned to damp ground, muting her footsteps. Clouds sailed in front of the quarter moon; he heard her suck in her breath. It was a sound women make when they are afraid or aroused, and it grated on his nerves. He ran his damp hands along his slacks, clenching and unclenching his fingers.

What has Janeshutz done here to pull the tension cord tighter? She has turned down the volume on the scene. Noise suggests companionship, life. Silence suggests death. Graves are silent. And so, where there had been at least the sound of leaves crackling beneath her feet, there is now "damp ground muting her footsteps." And what could be quieter than clouds sailing in front of the quarter moon? Our woman is frightened by the silence, so what does she do? She makes a noise, the sucking in of breath. But the noise grates on his nerves. More tension. How much does it grate on his nerves, we wonder. Enough to make him do "it" right now? Another writer might have our stalker do his deed now, but Janeshutz has control here and she's going to wring as much tension as she possibly can out of the scene. The trick is to loosen the cord just a bit, and she does that by breaking the frightening silence.

> The only clear sound now was a train in the distance, hurtling through the warm humid night. Denise, Denise, he thought, it could have been so different. If you'd been good. He dug his hand into his pocket and his fingers closed around the knife. It seemed warm, suddenly heavy, as if imbued with consciousness, with an awareness of what it would have to do.

Will the noise of the train save her, we wonder. Is it an interruption, does it suggest that there are people around who will scare off the murderer? What will happen when the sound of the train is gone and Denise is left alone in the silence?

> When the last of the train sounds left the air, she heard him and spun around, a hand flying dramatically to her heart.

Okay, this is it, we think. The tension has been all used up. We know the intent, we know the weapon, we know there is no way out for Denise. Can the tension be milked any further?

> Then she saw him and laughed nervously. "Christ, you scared the hell out of me." An admonishing tone, he thought, one he knew well.

Janeshutz has found a way to slightly loosen the cord again, before the final yank. We can relax, right? This is a friend of Denise's. She feels safe now, so why should we worry? Well, there is that knife in his pocket, and there are those thoughts he was having. Janeshutz has got us exactly where she wants us, tense because we think something awful is going to happen, but not completely sure. Is he going to murder Denise? That's the question that holds us to the page.

The answer is yes. Thirteen paragraphs later Janeshutz yanks the cord. The stalker does Denise in with the knife.

But we're only on page three. Is that the end of the tension? No. The next paragraph begins:

> A sense of urgency nibbled now at the edges of his mind as he thought of the lights that had been on in Denise's building. Suppose the other woman was already on the way to the parking lot.

Yes, indeed, a new set of worries for the reader. Will this guy get caught? Will the other woman show up? Will he murder her? Trish Janeshutz has put down one cord of tension and immediately begun to pull another taut. That's what she does throughout the book. There should always be unanswered questions. The reader should always be a little bit worried.

Afternoon Coffee Break

Time

I was sitting on a dock in Newburyport, Massachusetts, when I opened William Goldman's fine novel, *The Color of Light*. Goldman began, "Late on a late spring afternoon, Chub, ambling across the Oberlin campus, was astonished to see the girl of his dreams break into tears."

I didn't know why Goldman had used the word "late" twice in the first sentence. But I knew that Goldman is a pro and the words didn't just sprout there. He had planted them there for a reason.

I began thinking about writers and writing problems. Time is one of them. How to express it. Particularly, flashbacks.

Of course, I'm assuming that you have done a good deal of writing by now and you know about grammatical tense. But still many writers slip into time frames that confuse readers. Here's an example:

> When I was a kid I used to visit my grandmother every Thanksgiving. There would be gravy and stuffing and cranberry sauce and big bowls of cookies after dinner. When she took the turkey out of the oven some of the juices spilled on her foot and burned her badly. We called Doctor Peterson.

That's a pretty obvious example, but it makes the point. I switched from Thanksgiving in general to one Thanksgiving in particular without cueing the reader. I should have written, "One Thanksgiving when Grandma took the turkey out of the oven . . ." That would have smoothly transported the reader from the general time frame, which gave background information, to the specific time frame containing story information.

Here is another example that is typical of the ones I see in manuscripts:

> When Kimberly missed a behind-the-back scoop shot at the end of the first half, Miss Thompson had a fit. She was as emotional about the game as any male coach. She would whack her program into her hand over and over, kick the water bucket and scream,

"Fundamentals, fundamentals, how many times do I have to tell you girls, stick to the basics."

In this case, the writer is taking the reader out of a scene in order to give her some general information about Miss Thompson's behavior. Again the reader has not been cued, and the effect is confusing.

There are two ways to improve this. One would be to cue the reader that we are now going into Miss Thompson's general behavior. ("It was the same as always. Whenever a girl took a fancy shot Miss Thompson would have a fit," etc.) But the better way, most of the time, is not to generalize at all. Just show us Miss Thompson.

> Kimberly missed a behind-the-back scoop shot at the end of the half and Miss Thompson was on her feet screaming at Kimberly before the ball even hit the floor. She smashed her program into her hand. She kicked the water bucket and it went flying halfway across the court. "How many times do I have to tell you girls," she shouted. "Stick to the basics."

Unless you've created some special circumstances that would cause Miss Thompson to behave differently tonight, the reader will assume this is typical behavior. The scene will be stronger, Miss Thompson will be better characterized, and you will avoid making a time-frame mistake.

When you go back through your manuscript give special attention to all the words that indicate time, such as "when," "whenever," "later," and "often," as well as phrases that indicate time, such as "in the future" and "during this period." Ask yourself, is this sentence taking place at a different time from the previous sentence? Have I made that clear to the reader?

Also keep in mind that these time words are relative, so you want to make it clear which time frame your words are related to. Let's say, using Miss Thompson again, you write, "Later she calmed down and praised the girls for the good things they had done on the court." Which later? Later on the night that Kimberly missed the behind-the-back scoop shot, or later, in general, after she showed as much emotion as any male coach? If there's any room for doubt, make a specific reference. ("Later, though she still didn't understand why Kimberly would take such a reckless shot, Miss Thompson praised the girls for the good things they had done on the court.")

The time problem that seems to perplex the most writers is flashbacks. Many writers write awkward flashbacks because they are trying too hard to ease the reader into them. They try to take the reader through too many doors. Like this:

> When she left the studio that afternoon, Jennie noticed that the old man in the guard house was the same man who had greeted her on her first visit in 1979. He seemed no more impressed by her now that she was a big star, than he had been when she was a nervous extra coming in for a few days to work in anonymity.
>
> It had been summer then. She remembered that, though usually it was hard to remember seasons in L.A. where the changes were not as sharp as they were back home in Connecticut. Jenny glanced at the hills beyond the studio. L.A., she thought. What am I doing in a place like this? Back then she was driving a mustard-colored Mustang. Now she was being driven in a Mercedes. The Mustang had been a gift from her father. Dad, she thought. I'd better visit him soon. The old guard had waved her by and she had gone to Ted Donegan's office. He was the assistant director on that first film. He was a tall, red-headed man with a long red beard. "Perhaps I can get you something to say," he told her. It was her first break.

The problem here is that the writer is trying to bring the reader into the flashback through too many different doors. First there's the "same guard" door, then there's the "Mustang versus Mercedes" door, and the "star versus extra" and the "Dad who gave her the car versus the Dad she should visit soon." By presenting us with all these comparisons between then and now, the author is shouting, "Get ready. There's a flashback coming up." But instead of being helpful, he's just getting us confused. Getting into a flashback doesn't have to be a major production. The keys to a smooth flashback are 1. Use something memorable. 2. Go directly into the flashback. 3. Bring the reader out through the same door that led him in.

Something memorable can be an unusual word, an unusual combination of words, or something strongly visual.

Let's say your middle-aged couple is having a terrible fight, and they are talking about divorce. A good visual image to get you into flashback would be the wedding ring. The middle-aged husband storms out of the condominium. The wife yanks off her wedding ring and flings it on the floor.

It wasn't always like this, she thought, staring at the bright silver ring. (This is the door you are bringing the reader through.) When they were married in 1954 (Be specific about the time zone you are entering) they were as happy as two people could be. As soon as they drove away from the church they were making plans.

"I know it sounds crazy," Les said, "but I think I can make a go of this truck-pull thing. In the big cities thousands of people will come to see a truck pull."

Liz smiled. It was hard to imagine anybody paying to see a truck pull, but Les was so confident. She just knew he could do it, and she would be with him every step of the way.

Now you're into he flashback, 1954, and you can proceed forward from there for as long as you want. Forget that you are in flashback. It is irrelevant until you're ready to come out of it. Then, use the same door, the ring.

Les had been wrong about a lot of things, Liz thought, staring at the shiny silver ring she had tossed on the floor. But he had been right about those damn truck pulls. For some reason, people liked them. She picked up the ring, slipped it on her finger, and called her lawyer.

These were some of the things I thought about as I sat on the dock in Newburyport, Massachusetts. Then I got back into William Goldman's book. His second sentence begins a flashback. "He had fallen—quite literally—for B.J. Peacock twenty months before, his first day of orientation week freshman year." When I got to page eight I read this sentence. "And then late on that late spring afternoon Chub, ambling along, spotted them in the shadows of Tappan Square."

There it was again, that double *late* pulling me out of the flashback. Goldman had wanted me to notice the "late on that late" so that when I saw it again I would be reminded that Chub and I are not in the time and place of the flashback. We are on the Oberlin campus on that late spring afternoon. The double *late* was a guidepost to remind me of when and where I was standing in relation to Goldman's material. If he had written "late on a spring afternoon" it might have been too common for me to recognize when I saw it again. But "late on a late spring afternoon," like a dock in Newburyport, Massachusetts, is something you recognize when you see it a second time.

THREE

Viewpoint

By now in your writing career you are probably familiar with the concept of viewpoint. But that doesn't necessarily prevent you from making viewpoint mistakes. Most of the manuscripts I read have mistakes in viewpoint. I will give you some examples, but first, a quick refresher course in viewpoint.

Viewpoint is the place from which the reader views your story. If you imagine your story as a movie, then viewpoint is where you place the camera. Usually the camera is inside a character's head, looking out through his eyes. He is the viewpoint character and the camera records what he sees, smells, hears, and tastes. But the viewpoint is an emotional camera, not a mechanical one, and when you choose a viewpoint you are also choosing what the viewpoint character feels, thinks, and believes.

Viewpoint is generally discussed in the context of fiction because fiction presents far more opportunities for the writer to use different viewpoints and also far more chances to make viewpoint mistakes. For that reason most of this chapter will deal with fiction.

However, while viewpoint in nonfiction is relatively less important, it is still important, and we will discuss it. Also, keep in mind that when you write narrative nonfiction—that is, nonfiction that tells a story about characters, such as Truman Capote's *In Cold Blood,* all of the points about viewpoint in fiction apply to you.

There are many types of viewpoint, but a discussion of four of them should be enough to make the point.

Single Major Character Viewpoint

In this viewpoint the main character in a story is the only one who shares his thoughts with the reader. The reader knows what the main character sees, hears, smells, tastes, thinks, and feels, at the same time that the main character sees, hears, smells, tastes, thinks, and feels it. The reader has exactly the same access to information as the character, no more and no less, no sooner and no later.

This is the most commonly used viewpoint. It is the easiest to handle and it is the one that is closest to the reader's real-life experience. The single major character viewpoint can be written in the first person:

> When I got home from school this afternoon Ma was waiting for me in the kitchen.

> I was late, as usual. I had been kept after school for heaving a half-eaten apple into the girl's lavatory. Actually it was Marvin Silva who heaved the apple, but I didn't squeal on him, mainly because I didn't want to get beaten to a bloody pulp later on in the school yard.

Or the third person:

> When Brian got home from school his mother was waiting for him in the kitchen.

> Brian was late, as usual. He had been kept after school for heaving a half-eaten apple into the girl's lavatory. Actually it was Marvin Silva who heaved the apple, but Brian didn't squeal on him, mainly because Brian didn't want to get beaten to a bloody pulp later on in the school yard.

Those are main character viewpoints because all of the information is available to the main character. I would have violated viewpoint if I had written something like this:

Brian hadn't heaved the apple. He didn't know who did. Actually, it was Marvin Silva who had heaved the apple, and if Brian had known he probably wouldn't have squealed anyhow.

In that passage I have stepped out of Brian's viewpoint and shown information not available to him. The reason this can happen in fiction is that you have an "author," a person who has all the information, and a "character," a person who only has as much information as the author says he has. The break in viewpoint occurs when the character's viewpoint reveals something that only the author knows.

If you haven't got a tight grasp on what I just said, don't worry. I'll give you more examples later. I only mention it now to enhance a point about viewpoint in nonfiction.

The point is that in nonfiction you would almost never make that mistake, because in nonfiction there is usually only the writer-narrator, and no other character. So there is no "information gap." The author can only tell you what he knows.

Minor Character Viewpoint

In this viewpoint the camera is in the head of a minor character of the story. The rules are the same. The reader is entitled to no less and no more information than is available to the minor viewpoint character. This also can be written in the first or third person, but is more likely to be in the first person, as in *The Great Gatsby,* which is told by the minor character, Nick Carraway.

There was music from my neighbor's house through the summer nights. In his blue gardens men and girls came and went like moths among the whisperings and the champagne and the stars. At high tide in the afternoon I watched his guests diving from the tower of his raft, or taking the sun on the hot sand of his beach while his two motor boats slit the waters of the Sound, drawing aquaplanes over cataracts of foam. On weekends his Rolls Royce became an omnibus, bearing parties to and from the city between nine in the morning and long past midnight, while his station wagon scampered like a brisk yellow bug to meet all trains. And on Mondays eight servants, including an extra gardener, toiled all day with mops and scrubbing-brushes and hammers and garden-shears, repairing the ravages of the night before.

Carraway, the minor character, is telling the story, though he is not deeply involved in the events he describes.

If you read *The Great Gatsby* you come up with a lot of reasons why Fitzgerald might have chosen the minor character viewpoint. But one obvious one should suffice. By the end of the novel the main character, Gatsby, is dead. In fact, he was dead before Carraway began his narrative.

Omniscient Viewpoint

The omniscient viewpoint is like ABC TV's coverage of the Olympics. There are cameras everywhere. There are cameras in every character's mind, there are cameras that have X-ray lenses and can tell you what's going on on the other side of a wall or the other side of the world. There are even cameras that can look into the future.

With the omniscient viewpoint you can write things like:

> Unbeknownst to Michael he would in ten years time marry this girl he now treated so ungallantly. Not only that, but they would have two children, one of whom would grow up to be a lawyer in the prestigious firm of Discuillio and Piscitelli. In fact at that very moment, in a small town in Italy, Guido Discuillio, age ten, was playing with his Yo Yo in his room while his mother cooked pasta in the kitchen, and Guido thought, "When I grow up I will be a lawyer, and I will have my own office." Michael smiled at the girl, wondering if he would ever see her again.

As I say, in the omniscient viewpoint you can write something like that. I don't know why you would want to, but you could.

The omniscient viewpoint was more successful in fiction years ago when writers didn't have to compete with TV miniseries, movies, and major league baseball for attention. These days readers demand a tightly focused, compelling story, and with fiction they can rarely get that from the omniscient viewpoint.

I recommend that you avoid using the omniscient viewpoint in fiction, for two reasons.

One is that it is very difficult to master. There are too many options. Let's say you have your lovers, Jack and Jill, climbing a hill to fetch a pail of water. Well, what if Jack falls down and breaks his crown and goes tumbling down the hill? Do you stay in Jack's point of view and describe the nausea and the growing sense of terror he feels as he tumbles down the hill? Or do you stay in Jill's point of view and describe her sense of frustration over not knowing how she is going to get the pail of water down the hill by herself? And what if Jill goes tumbling after? Then what? Do you stay in her head and write about her feelings of self-loathing for making the same mistake Jack made? Or do you switch to Jack's viewpoint and describe the sight of Jill tumbling toward him as he lies injured at the bottom of the hill?

You could go crazy with all the options offered by omniscient viewpoint. And every time you make the wrong choice you will make the reader angry, because he will feel entitled to some other body of information which he would prefer to see.

The other reason that it is difficult to make omniscient viewpoint work successfully in fiction is that it is so different from the reader's real-life experience. In real life he can't see what's going on in Italy, or what will happen ten years from now, so it is more difficult to believe that it is possible in your story.

The reader of nonfiction will accept an omniscient viewpoint much more easily than the fiction reader, because he is not identifying with the narrator; he is listening to her. Also, a piece of nonfiction begins with the premise that the writer knows a lot about the subject at hand and will share whatever she thinks is important, no matter how much time or space it covers. Though the following passage would be extremely disturbing in fiction, the reader of nonfiction would accept it easily.

In the early 1890s Jesse W. Reno invented the first crude version of the escalator. By the 1930s the descendents of his device would be carrying people in banks, department stores, and subway stations all over the world. By the 1980s some escalators would be made with treads more than five feet wide, able to carry three persons standing side by side and move as many as 10,000 passengers per hour.

At about the same time that Reno was working on his invention, another inventor, Charles D. Seeberger, was developing a similar device, but it would be twenty years before the Otis elevator company would combine the best features of the Reno and Seeberger inventions to produce an escalator of the type we know today.

While the nonfiction reader will travel more easily through time and space, there is a limit to this sort of thing. You are still moving the reader around, and you have got to do it as seldom as possible.

Dual or Multiple Viewpoint

Years ago I read a novel called *John and Mary* in which half the chapters were written in John's viewpoint and half in Mary's. Though the author did switch from one mind to the other it is important to note that this is not omniscient viewpoint. It is single character viewpoint here, and another single character viewpoint there. It is not omniscient because at any given time in the story there is an implicit rule that says we can only see, hear, and feel what one character is seeing, hearing, feeling. With omniscient viewpoint the rule is we can see anything at any time. With *John and Mary* the author alternated between two different single character viewpoints. That is called dual viewpoint. It could have been three or four different characters and that would be multiple viewpoint. Books have been written in which every chapter is a new character's viewpoint. And the viewpoint change doesn't have to occur at the beginning of the chapter, either. It can occur within a chapter, or within a short story. So you can see that avoiding the omniscient viewpoint is not all that limiting. By creatively using the single character viewpoint with different characters at different times, you can cover a good deal of ground. But beware. It is when writers indiscriminately use the multiple viewpoint unknowingly, unnecessarily, or ineffectively that they make a mess of things.

If you use the dual viewpoint, balance the two viewpoints. If you write Chapter One in Jack's viewpoint and Chapter Two in Jill's viewpoint and then Chapters Three through Seventeen in Jack's viewpoint, the reader will be disturbed by the question, "Why isn't he writing in Jill's viewpoint?" since you've already told her that such a thing is possible. Any time you announce a rule of the game, such as, "We are allowed to see into two different minds," you are obliged to use it from time to time. Otherwise you leave the impression that the rule was not made for the good of the story, but simply to solve some technical problem you had in Chapter Two. This, of course, applies to multiple viewpoint as well as dual viewpoint.

Viewpoint Mistakes

Making a viewpoint mistake means simply that you have yanked the reader out of her comfortable position without giving her something in return that's worth the disturbance you've caused. Sometimes you switch viewpoint without knowing it, and sometimes you know you've done it but you don't realize how much trouble you've caused.

Just remember that every time you change viewpoint you disturb the reader. In effect, you have put her in place and are showing her something when suddenly you grab her by the shoulders and spin her around to look at something else. Of course she's annoyed. Wouldn't you be?

The viewpoint change is not so jarring when it occurs at the end of a scene. The reader is not expecting to be moved, but at least she's expecting to see something different. And when the viewpoint change occurs at the start of a new chapter there is even less disturbance, because the reader believes she has seen all there is to see from her particular angle, and so she is ready to look elsewhere.

But when you change viewpoints in the middle of a scene, while the reader is entranced by what she is watching, you disturb her greatly and if you do it often she will forsake you. So viewpoint rule number one is: never change viewpoints when you don't have to. And rule number two is: if you change viewpoint make sure you reward the reader for her troubles, with an exciting new scene or chapter, or some compelling new information. (This, incidentally, applies to every aspect of your writing. Never disturb the reader without giving something in return. There must always be a payoff.)

An Example

My friend Bonnie Ireland in Dallas is a good fiction writer. She sent me one book, which I think is close to being publishable. Then she sent me *The Quality of Mercy,* which I have just begun. Though I've only read a few pages I can see that the greatest problem with the book is going to be viewpoint. So let's get to work on it. Here is the first page and a half.

> The Reverend Guntree's fist punctuated the last words of his sermon with a magnificent wallop. Vibrations resounded back and forth across the heavy wooden beams above, even the pedestal platform on which the Reverend stood, shook and rattled so that

the metal parasol over his head made strange jangling sounds. Everyone in the congregation jumped. Those who had momentarily closed their eyes opened them in frantic haste, fearing the anger of God had fallen upon them. No one, but no one, slept while the Reverend was delivering his Sunday morning message to the little town of Penance.

At this point Bonnie has not yet committed herself to a viewpoint. We know that we are somewhere in the church, but all of the information in the first paragraph is available to anybody in the church.

Suddenly all sounds came to an end. The pulpit righted itself with a final lurch, and in the silence Reverend Guntree's dark piercing eyes swept across every pew and connected his congregation.

Okay, now we have eliminated Reverend Guntree as the viewpoint character. By showing us his dark piercing eyes, Bonnie has put us in the audience looking toward Reverend Guntree. But where exactly in the audience are we?

Ellie Quinceblossom saw the Reverend's eyes light on her. She gave a slight cough and blinked her eyelids fast. Lifting a plump arm encased in black lace, she fiddled with the grey curls at the nape of her neck and giggled nervously. Then she looked hard at the back of Willie Neff who sat in front of her.

Now the viewpoint has been established. The camera is inside Ellie Quinceblossom's head. From here we can see the back of Willie Neff's head, the Reverend, the pulpit, etc. This is fine. No viewpoint mistakes yet. We should not be told anything about what's behind Ellie, unless the author tells us that Ellie turned around.

Willie was beginning to think the Reverend was looking at him. He twitched his unruly moustache and could feel the red glow coming higher and higher up his neck until his cheeks bloomed like one of the red roses in his garden.

There it is, the first change in viewpoint, and it's jarring. We had just gotten settled inside Ellie's head, when we were yanked out of it and pushed one row forward into the head of Willie Neff, where we were given information that was unavailable to Ellie.

But the Reverend was wondering how he could get Ellie to pay another penance because the Altar Cloth was almost worn out and no one in his congregation could tat or crochet like Miss Ellie Quinceblossom.

Just as we are catching our breath from the first movement we are yanked out of Willie's head, brought all the way up to the pulpit, and spun around so that we are now facing the congregation, looking out through the eyes of the Reverend. This is very disturbing.

Suddenly, out of the silence, the huge wooden doors at the front of the church opened with a series of squeaks. Who would dare come in at the end of his sermon? All in Penance were accounted for . . . he had seen to that with his own eyes.

Okay, we are still in the Reverend's point of view, looking toward the front of the church. Maybe we can get comfortable now and watch the story unfold.

The Reverend's face turned ashen. There was shock and utter bewilderment expressed on his rugged features as he looked beyond the congregation. With one accord all eyes watched and wondered.

By showing us the Reverend's face, the author has yanked us out of the Reverend's point of view and back into the audience looking up toward him. How else could we see his rugged features? This is the third viewpoint change and we are still in the first scene. As readers we are getting yanked all over the place, and we're getting dizzy.

Bonnie's mistakes here are typical. She's writing her scene from up in the sky, instead of grounding herself someplace and describing what she sees. She should imagine herself as a big heavy movie camera someplace in that church and then she will notice how often she is moving the camera.

So how can she fix this? Does she have to get rid of most of the information because she can't switch viewpoints? No. She just has to decide who the viewpoint character is, and then reveal that information in a way that would be available to that character.

We'll talk later about how you decide who should be the viewpoint character, but let's assume for a moment that Bonnie decides that Ellie Quinceblossom should be her viewpoint character. With only Ellie's perceptions available to her, Bonnie could rewrite like this:

Ellie Quinceblossom sat quietly in her pew and listened as the Reverend Guntree's fist punctuated the last words of his sermon with a magnificent wallop. Vibrations resounded back and forth across the heavy wooden beams above; even the pedestal platform on which the Reverend stood, shook and rattled so that the metal parasol over his head made strange jangling sounds. It seemed to Ellie that everyone in the congregation jumped. Even those who had momentarily closed their eyes opened them in frantic haste, perhaps fearing the anger of God had fallen upon them. No one, but no one, slept while the Reverend was delivering his Sunday morning message to the little town of Penance.

Suddenly all sounds came to an end. The pulpit righted itself with a final lurch, and in the silence Reverend Guntree's dark piercing eyes swept across every pew and connected his congregation.

When the Reverend's eyes lighted on her, Ellie gave a slight cough and blinked her eyelids fast. Lifting a plump arm encased in black lace, she fiddled with the curls at the back of her neck. She imagined them as the blonde they used to be, rather than the grey they had become. She giggled nervously. Then she looked hard at the back of Willie Neff, who sat in front of her.

Willie was twitching at his moustache the way he always did whenever he thought the Reverend was looking at him. A red glow of embarrassment rose along the back of his neck and flooded his cheeks. By God, he's blooming like one of the roses in his garden, Ellie thought.

Glancing away from Willie and back to the pulpit, Ellie noticed that the Altar Cloth was worn and tattered. Perhaps she could make another, Ellie thought. She sat up a little straighter in her pew, thinking there was still no one in the congregation who could tat or crochet as well as she could.

Again her thoughts wandered to Willie Neff, and she was invaded by that sense of sadness that often came with thoughts of Willie. There was a time when she thought Willie would ask her to marry, but he never had and she never knew why. It would have been a beautiful wedding right here in this church. She began to sketch the details in her mind, when suddenly the silence of the church was broken by a series of squeaks. Ellie turned and stared at the huge wooden doors at the front of the church. They were opening. Who would dare come in at the end of Reverend Guntree's sermon? Ellie looked around. It seemed that every member of the congregation was already in church.

She looked at the pulpit. The Reverend's face had turned ashen. There was shock and utter bewilderment expressed on his rugged features as he looked out at the congregation.

Testing for Viewpoint

If you are still not certain about viewpoint, you'll find it safe to write in the first person. It would be difficult to unknowingly violate viewpoint while writing in the first person. If you have written something in the third person and you are not certain whether or not you have violated viewpoint you can usually flush out the mistakes by rewriting in the first person. Here is an example.

> He was called Gimpel the fool. He didn't think of himself as a fool. On the contrary. But that's what folks called him. They gave him the name while he was still in school. He had seven names in all: imbecile, donkey, flax-head, dope, glump, ninny, and fool. The last name stuck. What did his foolishness consist of? He was easy to take in. They said "Gimpel, you know the Rabbi's wife has been brought to childbed?" So he skipped school. Well, it turned out to be a lie. How was he supposed to know? She hadn't had a big belly. But he never looked at her belly. Was that really so foolish? The gang laughed and hee-hawed, stomped and danced and chanted a good-night prayer. And instead of the raisins they give when a woman's lying in, they stuffed his hand full of goat turds. He was no weakling. If Gimpel slapped someone the victim would see all the way to Cracow. But he really was not a slugger by nature. He thinks to himself: Let it pass. So they take advantage of him. Though Gimpel didn't know it, a young girl by the name of Rachel thought he was not such a fool. He had never seen Rachel. She was a slender girl with long black hair and brown eyes that shone as if they had been polished.

That passage, except for the last three sentences, is my rewrite of the beginning of Isaac Bashevis Singer's short story, "Gimpel the Fool." Singer wrote the story in the first person, but I have changed it to the third person and with those last three sentences I have violated the viewpoint. If you had written that you might not have noticed the break in viewpoint, but if you rewrote it in the first person the violation would jump right out at you.

> I am Gimpel the fool. I don't think of myself as a fool. On the contrary. But that's what folks call me. They gave me the name while I was still in school. I had seven names in all: imbecile, donkey, flax-head, dope, glump, ninny, and fool. The last name stuck. What did my foolishness consist of? I was easy to take in. They said, "Gimpel, you know the Rabbi's wife has been brought to childbed?" So I skipped school. Well, it turned out to be a lie. How was I supposed to know? She hadn't had a big belly. But I never looked at her belly. Was that really so foolish? The gang laughed and hee-hawed, stomped and danced and chanted a good-night prayer. And instead of the raisins they give when a woman's lying in, they stuffed my hand full of goat turds. I was no weakling. If I slapped someone he'd see all the way to Cracow. But I'm really not a slugger by nature. I think to myself: Let it pass. So they take advantage of me. Though I didn't know it a young girl by the name of Rachel thought I was not such a fool. I had never seen Rachel. She was a slender girl with long black hair and brown eyes that shone as if they had been polished.

The contradiction of Gimpel's saying that he has never seen a girl and then describing her is a mild shock and you would notice it in rereading your manuscript. That shock is what your reader feels every time you change viewpoint.

Choosing Viewpoint

Remember the Jack and Jill story? Who would you choose for the viewpoint character? Would you use dual viewpoint? Would you use omniscient viewpoint and write something like, "Poor Jack did not know it, but soon he would fall down and break his crown." Would you use a minor character viewpoint? "I saw Jack and Jill going up the hill that fateful day. They had a pail with them. Apparently they were going to fetch some water."

The number of choices can paralyze you at the typewriter. I have a novel-in-progress called *Local References* which I have been dragging out of my closet once a year since 1967. The reason the book has never been finished is that I have never been able to stick to a decision about its viewpoint.

The viewpoint decision can be maddening because as soon as you choose a viewpoint you have to make sacrifices. Some clever piece of description has got to go because it describes something your viewpoint character has never seen. A witty bit of dialogue has got to bite the dust because nobody ever said it to your viewpoint character, and he would never say something like that himself. And so forth. But that's the way it goes in the writing game. You've got to put your ego aside and make decisions that are best for your readers.

One thing always to keep in mind is that you want to keep things as uncomplicated as possible. In a short story, for example, always use a single character viewpoint unless you have an extremely compelling reason for doing something else. The scope of a short story is rarely wide enough to support anything else.

A careful analysis of what your story is really about will help you to choose a point of view. Ask yourself, which character has the problem that must be solved in this story? Who will be changed the most by the events of this story? Who has the ability to solve the problems of the story? Whose behavior best demonstrates the message of your story? If you are writing a mystery, then choose a viewpoint character who can't have all the facts until the end of the story.

Also, in choosing a viewpoint, consider the reader. Usually when we write a short story for a magazine we write the story first and then figure out what magazine we want to send it to. But if you know what magazine you want to sell to before you've decided on viewpoint, then ask yourself who the magazine reader will identify with. If you are writing the Jack and Jill story for *Redbook,* then Jill should probably be the viewpoint character. If you are writing it for *Playboy* then Jack will make a better viewpoint character. If you are writing a novel for men and women then you may want to have at least one male and one female viewpoint character. If your story is about two brothers and one of them is a psycho murderer, your reader will probably identify more easily with the other brother as the viewpoint character.

If you've done all this and it is still not obvious what viewpoint you should use, or who the viewpoint character should be, begin the story in different viewpoints and see which one feels right.

Choosing a Viewpoint Character in Nonfiction

I said earlier that the reason there were few viewpoint switches in nonfiction was that nonfiction usually does not have a writer-narrator and a character. However, the concept of character viewpoint is still valid in nonfiction for a couple of reasons.

One reason is that sometimes you relate anecdotes within your article, little stories that illustrate some point, and in writing the anecdote you have to wisely choose the viewpoint character just as you would with any other story.

If you are writing an article about how employees at nuclear power plants can take some responsibility for their own safety and you have an anecdote about the time there was almost a catastrophe because an employee refused to take orders from a government inspector, you will probably tell the anecdote from the point of view of the employee. If your article is about how difficult it is for government inspectors to enforce regulations you would probably write the anecdote from the point of view of the inspector.

The other reason that you have to think about character viewpoint in your nonfiction is that, even though nonfiction doesn't have a writer *and* a character, it has a writer who *is* a character. Remember that viewpoint is an emotional camera, and it has an attitude as well as a placement. At first glance the "attitude" of the nonfiction narrator might seem to be a totally different meaning of the word "viewpoint" from the one that we have been discussing. But it's not. "Attitude toward material" is another way of saying "viewpoint character." Even though you are almost always the narrator of your nonfiction you take on a specific personality for each article or book. If you regard that personality as the viewpoint character then you will not make the mistake of violating viewpoint by switching from a humorous character to a solemn one or an impartial character to a biased one. You will stick to the viewpoint character, the personality you've created.

Here are excerpts from two different articles. After you've read each, try to describe the narrator. Is he hip? Is he cynical? Is he funny? Is he serious? How old is he? Describe the way you see him.

> In days gone by it was the imagined crack of a bat launching a baseball out of Yankee Stadium that kept many a young fellow awake half the night with visions of future heroics. Today, it is just as often the relentless throbbing twang of a plugged-in guitar that

gluts his imagination. Times change. Junior wants to be a rock star.

But just as those juicy home run balls were never going to be served up easily by a sympathetic pitcher, rocking and rolling for dough will not come without years of frustration and work. There's a lot more to it these days than just learning three chords and looking pretty. It's not simply a case of "git yourself a gitar" as the lyrics of an old rock song tell us. The competition is fierce, the dues are heavy, and the payoff is meager for all but the very good and the very fortunate.

For starters, the dimensions of the term "rock and roll" have been extended to include just about anything a rock and roll band feels like doing. These days, they feel like doing jazz, funky, R&B, choreography, comedy, and composing.

We say the name Robert Goddard and we envision a bespectacled man with a mustache, standing in an Auburn field shooting rockets up to heights considered shallow by today's standards. We know that what he did was important, but like most great men of science, Goddard's image has become mechanized, screwed onto our imaginations like a cog in the technology he pioneered. We forget that behind the calculations and the experiments there breathed a flesh-and-blood man with other interests, with hopes and feelings. We forget that the man grew from a wistful Worcester lad who liked to fly kites and could gaze for hours at the flight of birds, and that it was those feelings that inspired his scientific achievements.

In the case of Robert Hutchings Goddard, the achievements are numerous. His work laid the foundation on which today's space adventures are built. He tested the first rocket engines to use liquid fuel. In 1929 he sent up the first instrument-carrying rocket. He accumulated more than two hundred rocketry-related patents and though his work was largely ignored here in America, it was basic to the weaponry developed by Germany in the 1930s and during World War II.

Have you described the two narrators? Are they somewhat different?

I am the narrator in both, and I wrote both articles during the same month in 1978. But because of differences in the material and the audience I have brought different parts of myself to each story. My attitude in each story has become my viewpoint character.

Describing the Viewpoint Character

Do you remember Reverend Guntree's dark piercing eyes? Do you remember where you were when you saw them? In a pew looking toward the Reverend Guntree, of course. If you were inside his head . . . his point of view . . . you would not be able to see the color of his eyes, or the shape of his nose or anything else about his face or hair. This is a problem with character viewpoint. In order to describe a character, it seems, you have to violate viewpoint by yanking the reader out of the character's head, and turning her around so that she can stare back at the character and see what he looks like. Or, of course, you could always do something like this:

> As she strolled along main street that morning Beatrice caught a glimpse of herself in the wide window of Lincoln Drugs. She saw that her hips had widened slightly, no doubt from the rich food she had been wolfing down all through her California vacation. As usual, the mannish turn of her shoulders made her look not as feminine as she would like. But the sparkle was still there in her blue eyes, which coruscated like distant lakes in the sunshine, and her long blonde hair, freshly washed, seemed especially lustrous today. What about my nose, she wondered, poking at it as she stared at her reflection. Is it as crooked as I think? She smiled to study her teeth. They were her best feature. People said she had teeth like Farrah Fawcett. As Beatrice stood looking forlornly at her forgettable figure she wished she had a lot of other things like Farrah Fawcett.

You could do that. But don't. And don't have your viewpoint character looking in mirrors, the placid surfaces of crystal clear ponds, or the shiny fenders of recently waxed Oldsmobiles to see what she looks like. The only good thing that can be said about that sort of thing is that it shows that the writer is sensitive to point of view, and is trying not to violate it. The problem with this reflection business is that it is overused and it has the same effect as a cliché, a stereotyped character, or a predictable plot. The reader recognizes what is going on. He sees the writer at work, and the writer comes off looking like an amateur.

So what can you do? Well, I talked to my friend Gary Goshgarian about that. Goshgarian is a novelist, and he is also a professor at Northeastern University where he teaches creative writing. Gary, I said, what about describing the viewpoint character?

"Well," he said, "of course there's always the old mirror trick, or the reflection in the store window. But no writer with any sense should try those. I see a lot of that sort of thing and it never works well; it's always awkward. But there are a number of effective ways. One is to show other people's reactions. If women glance back at a guy when he's walking down the street, then we can surmise that he is handsome, sexy, whatever. If people look up at him, he's tall. If they look down, he's short. So the reaction of other characters tells us a lot. And there are the character's own little activities. If he gets food on his moustache then we know he has a moustache.

"But even better, I think, is to find a way to make the reader believe that the character is thinking about his appearance. You can't just say, 'As Dan walked past the Arlington Street subway station he thought about his red hair and the fact that he was only five foot six.' That's too heavy-handed. But if you can find an emotional connection you can get the information across without disturbing the reader. Let's say the story is about Sam's relationship with his father, and his trying to live up to his father's image. You might write something like, 'Sam's hair was not as red as his father's and at five foot six, he was not even as tall as his dad. God, he thought, I haven't measured up to the old man in any way.' This, to me, would not be a break in viewpoint, because we haven't seen Sam by jumping outside and looking at him. We have seen him by listening to thoughts that we believe he would have."

Follow Goshgarian's advice and also keep in mind that a precise visual description of your main character is not as important as you might think, and often is detrimental. After all, your reader is identifying with this person, and doesn't want to be reminded too much of the differences. The reader's strongest image of your character does not come from what you say he looks like. It comes from the character's actions in the story. If Donald has a hard time opening a jar of pickles in the first scene, can't seem to get his belt tight enough in the second scene, and gets tossed around by a gust of wind in the third scene, the reader will have a much more vivid image of him than if you had spent fifty words telling her how skinny and frail Donald is.

The Deeper Meaning of Viewpoint

In this chapter I have talked mostly about viewpoint as camera placement. From where is the reader seeing the story? But when you choose a character's viewpoint you are choosing his entire view of the world, and that includes his prejudices, his ignorance, his fears, etc. Character viewpoint is not objective. It is constantly influenced by the nature of the character.

"Viewpoint is slippery," Gary Goshgarian said. "It's a hard concept to get hold of. But the writer has to, because it is all tied up in the contracts he makes with the reader. The writer has to remember that viewpoint includes the character's perception of the world, and the writer must write out of that perception, not his own."

Here, for example, is what the inner city neighborhood looks like when ten-year-old Tommy goes to visit his cousin Cliffy for a month in the summer.

> It made his neighborhood in Lancaster seem pretty dull by comparison. In Lancaster there was nothing to do in the summer, but here there were hundreds of things. People left things right out on the sidewalk and after just one walk around the block with Cliffy, Tommy had collected an old faucet, half of a comic book, and the knob from a car's gearshift.
>
> There weren't just a few houses, like in Lancaster. There were dozens of them on every block, and in one of the back yards Tommy saw an old tub that would make a great ship when he and Cliffy played pirates. The houses were tall and close together and between them were secret passageways where Tommy could hide when he and Cliffy's friends had water pistol wars. The back yards were small squares of dirt surrounded by wooden fences, but almost every fence had a slat missing, so you could take a shortcut to the construction field two blocks away.
>
> A lot of the kids had scooters and Tommy was going to learn how to make one out of wooden crates, planks from torn-down houses, and broken roller skates. This place was fantastic.

That passage is written in Tommy's viewpoint and we can imagine that it is from a story about a boy who spends a month at his cousin's in the city. But what if it's really a story about a woman who sends her son

174 / Beyond Style

to live in the city for a month? What if her name is Ellen and she's the viewpoint character? What would the camera see then?

> After her goodbyes to Tommy, Ellen stood out on the sidewalk in front of her sister's house. She wanted Tommy to experience new things, new people, but she wasn't at all sure that she wanted her son living in a place like this for a whole month. Things were not green and spacious here the way they were in Lancaster. The houses were crowded close together, with squalid little alleys between them, and the streets were littered with junk. A breeze tossed a torn old comic book across her feet. A few feet away, just lying on the sidewalk, was a discarded faucet with a jagged edge that could quickly cut a child's finger, and beyond that a piece from an abandoned car, debris dropped anywhere by people so impoverished that they no longer took pride in their surroundings.
>
> In one back yard an abandoned tub sat rusting in the summer heat. Ellen could just imagine how easily it might tip and fall if kids played in it. "Watch out, I got no brakes," someone shouted, and a little boy zoomed past her on a homemade wooden scooter. The people here were too poor even to buy bicycles for their children. What a dreadful place to have to raise a kid.

Form

So folks, here we go again, perplexed yet ever-so-hopeful writers diving head first into a morass of writing terms that rarely mean the same thing twice, terms that twitch and shiver in our mind like globules of mercury. Form and content, for heaven's sake! Who can even be sure where one picks us up and the other lets us off? A morass? No, a mirage would be more like it—yes, a mirage, from the distance looking for all the world like something we can lay our hands on, we can measure, we can weigh, we can seriously discuss . . . and yet from two feet away containing no more heft than your average ball of dust. And yet, hearty searchers for truth that we are, we pounce on it enthusiastically, and once again we are no more successful than if we were wrestling with a cloud.

What's wrong with that lead?

Is the *form*, the writing good? Yes, it's colorful, it's lively, it has strong verbs and some vivid images. Is the *content*, the subject, appropriate? Certainly; the paragraph is about form and content in writing, and this is a book about writing. So the form and the content are both good.

What's wrong is that they are not good for each other. They are not compatible.

The style of the paragraph is loose, almost zany. It has the personality of a carnival. It spreads all over the place like a puddle. It would be perfectly appropriate for your first-person account of a drunken escapade at Mardi Gras. The reader would come along for the ride and he wouldn't care much where you took him as long as it was fun.

But the content of that first paragraph is writing instruction. It is intended for a reader who cares very much, a reader who picked up this book to get specific information. Metaphorically speaking, the reader of this chapter is not going along for a ride; he is sitting quietly and listening intently. He is looking for instruction, not entertainment, and he wants definite points, not implications and vague allusions. So the form of the first paragraph is not wrong; it's just wrong for this particular book. Form and content must be compatible, and that's what this chapter is about.

After a story or an article has been written, separating form from content even long enough to define them is difficult. But that's OK. Form and content should be interwoven so that they appear to be inevitably bound for each other, like two perfect, inseparable lovers. The good story or article looks as if it could have been written no other way.

Content

When you think about the content of your story or article, think about just one thing: information. Whether it comes in the form of fiction or nonfiction, fact or opinion, description or characterization, the content of your story is information. That is the only clay you have to mold. Everything else is form.

At first glance it might seem that information is immutable and form is merely the frame you use to display it. This is a reasonable way to look at a story before you write it. But once you commit information to any form, the information and the form become the same thing. Tickle one and the other will giggle.

Compare:

Wade Boggs did hit a home run, but he struck out three times.

with

Wade Boggs did strike out three times, but he hit a home run.

By changing the form, you also slightly alter the content, the information.

Every time you change the form of your writing, even one word, you change the content, sometimes subtly, sometimes drastically. Your job as a writer is to make sure that form and content are on the same team. They should be working with each other, not against each other.

While content has only one meaning, form has several. The form of your story can mean the type of story, the length of the story, the format, the slant, or—and most important—the style in which it is written. I'll discuss them, starting with the easy ones.

Form, Meaning Story Type

By story type, I mean novel, short story, nonfiction book, magazine article, poem, whatever it is called. The wise choice of which form to use for your content is almost always obvious.

If, for example, you are trapped in an elevator for two hours with Jack Nicholson and he spends the time telling you about his life and career, it becomes immediately clear that your best shot at selling this material is in the form of a magazine article, an interview-profile of Jack Nicholson. Only the most optimistic or inexperienced writer would expect to turn it into a publishable poem, a short story, or a book about people who have gotten trapped in elevators with celebrities.

Because the decision on type of story is so obvious, you may not think of it as a decision at all, until it turns out to be the wrong decision.

One of the most common comments from editors rejecting book proposals is, "I think this would work better as a magazine article." That usually means that the material is not compelling enough to attract $15 from a book buyer (or even $3.95 for a paperback) or that there's not enough material to justify an entire book. The attempt to fatten magazine article material into a book is the most common wrong decision about type of story. Not every subject is suitable for a book. Most articles you read could not become books. (Though it's common for an article to become a chapter in a book or for a series of articles to become a book.) Few people would buy a book titled *How to Save on Heating Oil Costs This Winter* or *Elgin, Illinois: Vacation Paradise*, but those are perfectly appropriate ideas for articles.

Form, Meaning Length

Obviously, a decision to put your information in the form of a book instead of an article is a decision about length. But within the "type of story" categories, length is also an important form and content consideration.

The length of the story must be appropriate for the scope of the material. You could write a four thousand-word article, "The Boston Celtics: The Greatest Dynasty in Sports," but if your article is about "The Boston Celtics: Their Greatest Game," fifteen hundred words would probably be the most you could write without repeating yourself and putting your reader to sleep.

The length must also be appropriate for the nature of the material. A very thin book on weight loss could have a positive effect on readers. On the other hand, the writer who uses three thousand words to write an article called, "How to Explain Anything in Five Hundred Words or Less," will be lucky if he has any readers left at the end of the article.

Form, Meaning Format

The format of your story
is the arrangement, the layout
And at a glance you can see
that the format of a poem
is the wrong form
  for the content
    Of this story.

However, you have seen many articles in which the writer made his format compatible with his content.

Here are some examples:

1. A profile of a famous playwright, written in three acts.
2. An article about the post office written in the form of a letter.
3. A story about a space mission written in the form of a countdown.

While these devices are obvious, and sometimes distracting, they do a lot of good work. They give the reader a sharper picture of the material. Don't try to do something like this every time you write, but with each story consider the possibility that there might be a format which would enhance the material.

Form, Meaning Slant

So far I have discussed the connection between form and content in ways that are obvious to your reader. She can see easily that your post office article is in the form of a letter, etc. But the less obvious merging of form and content is far more important. And form, meaning slant, is one of those less obvious connections.

There are hundreds of ways you can use slant to enhance your content (or misuse it, to the detriment of your content) but I will discuss just three to make the point.

1. A viewpoint slant.

Let's say that one day you get lucky and an editor from *Sports Illustrated* calls and offers you a couple of thousand bucks to write a piece on "A Day at the Kentucky Derby."

"Fly to Louisville," he says, "talk to the Churchill Downs management, talk to the Louisville town fathers, talk to the spectators, the jockeys, the trainers, the horse owners, and the people in the city."

But right after he hangs up, your hot water heater explodes, your husband runs off with a nurse, your dog Buster has puppies, and there's a strike at the airport. So, for various other reasons you don't get to Louisville until four hours before the race. By that time the managers are too busy to talk to you, the spectators are too rowdy, and the town fathers are all three sheets to the wind on mint juleps. In fact, the only sober people who will talk to you are the jockeys. So you whip out your tape recorder, interview six jockeys, catch the race, and fly home to feed the puppies.

Hmmm. The form you had planned was a broad view of the Kentucky Derby as a big Louisville event. But the actual content of the material you have is a bunch of interviews with jockeys. If you try to pass that off as a broad view of the Derby, your form and content will not be compatible. The reader will be annoyed because he has been promised one thing and given another. He will say to his wife, "Gee Marian, this is a lousy article. All this woman talks about is the jockeys."

You have to make the form, meaning slant, harmonious with the content of what you actually have, not with what you wish you had. What do you do?

Well, you could change the article from "A Day at the Derby" to "Jockeys of the Derby," but you'd get in trouble with your editor, who asked you to write an article about the Derby, not about jockeys. There is another solution. Find the best viewpoint. Find the imaginary place from which you have gotten the best view of the Derby. In this case the jockeys offer the best viewpoint. You didn't talk to everybody so don't write from everybody's point of view. You talked to the jockeys, so write about what they think on Derby Day. Their viewpoint is your content, so their viewpoint should be your form.

2. A metaphor slant.

An example should suffice here. In a *Boston Globe* article, Michael Blowen wrote about director Barry Levinson. For his slant, Blowen used a baseball metaphor—specifically, the progress from the minor leagues to the major leagues. Blowen's first paragraph:

> Barry Levinson, wearing a New York Knights baseball jacket, strides into the lobby of the fashionable Mayfair Hotel on Park Avenue. The writer-director, previously known for the $5 million movie, *Diner,* is publicizing his new film, *The Natural,* a $20 million all-star movie starring Robert Redford. Welcome to the big leagues.

Blowen does not take a hard swing at his baseball metaphor, but does from time to time put his words in baseball terminology. The metaphor works well and holds the piece together. The reason it works well is that much of Blowen's content concerns *The Natural,* a baseball movie. The baseball metaphor form is compatible with the baseball content, but Blowen went easy on the metaphor because baseball is only part of the content. If the film had no baseball content, the form would not have worked because the reader would be nagged by the question, "Why is he using a baseball metaphor for a movie director?" And if Blowen had used a football metaphor (Barry Levinson scores a touchdown with *The Natural*) the piece would have looked ridiculous.

3. A handicap slant.

Often, after you've gathered material, you will regard some aspect of a writing project as a handicap. It might be a short deadline or limited space or an editor who hates your guts. But often the handicap is the lack of certain information. It is content that you don't have, and we'll call it "negative content." If you ignore the negative content and proceed as if you had the information, you are going to end up with a hole in your story and angry readers will say things like, "Hey Marian, this writer is a real bozo; she's writing this article about the Kentucky Derby and she doesn't even say how much money was bet."

To eliminate the hole and make form compatible with negative content, you must neutralize the negative content or make it work for you. Putting it another way, you must make your handicap irrelevant or turn it into a strength.

To make your handicap irrelevant, find out what you don't have, then create a story that wouldn't include it even if you did have it. If you've gathered a lot of information about ice cream but you can't find out how it's made or who invented it, write a piece called, "Ten Odd Facts About Ice Cream" and there won't be any hole. If you've interviewed several people about religious views and abortion but didn't talk to any members of the clergy, write "Religion and Abortion: the Layperson's Perspective," and no one will fault you for leaving out ministers, priests, and rabbis.

Those are examples of form that makes the negative content irrelevant. Here's an example of form that makes negative content into a strength.

Denise Worrell wrote an article about Michael Jackson for *Time* magazine. Her handicap was one that many writers might regard as fatal: Jackson, living a reclusive life, wasn't giving interviews. If Worrell had ignored the fact that there was no Michael Jackson presence in her story, there would have been a hole. The reader would have felt defrauded and he would have said to his wife, "Gee, Marian, this woman is writing about Michael Jackson and she didn't even interview Jackson. Can you imagine?"

So Worrell made her form compatible with her negative content. She worked with the slant, "Michael Jackson is a recluse." In her article she writes about her visit to the Jackson house and her interview with Joe Jackson, Michael's father. She includes the information and anecdotes that a Michael Jackson fan would want to read. And through it all she creates a strong sense of Michael Jackson not being there. She doesn't have his presence so she turns his absence into information about him. When Worrell finally spoke to Michael, it was only long enough to say hello.

> We back out of the room and Joe shuts the door. We walk away and he says, "Michael has a friend over. He isn't about to give any interviews. You got pretty close, though."

And at the end of her piece, after she leaves the Jackson house, Worrell writes:

This time the cab gets past the gate, which click closed behind us. On the street are two police cars and a group of teenage girls hanging out, hoping for a glimpse of Michael.

It's the perfect ending for her slant. She has turned the weakness of her content into the strength of her form. Nobody would expect her to interview Michael Jackson for an article that says Michael Jackson doesn't give interviews. Perfect.

Form, Meaning Style

Style in writing is not what you write, but how you write it. Style is sculpture, not clay. Of all the definitions of form in writing, style is the most important. Style can help you the most by being compatible with your content, and it can hurt you the most by being in conflict with your content. That is why I used an example of the wrong style to begin this chapter. Do you remember that first paragraph, the one that had the style of a vacation but the content of a classroom?

To use style in harmony with content, you must have a definite sense of who the reader is and why he is reading. If he has picked up your article on how to fix toasters, he is looking for information, nothing else. If he has come home from work and picked up your novel he might be looking for some poetic language that will lift him above the mundane world of the sneaker factory outlet where he works, so your style might be rich and musical.

Let us consider, as an example, the difference between a private detective novel and a category romance novel.

Content for the private detective novel reader is "what happens next, and then what happens." That is why most successful private detective novels are written in a style that is fast-paced and to the point. Something is almost always happening. Consider this opening from *Fletch's Fortune,* part of the highly successful Fletch series by Gregory McDonald:

"C.I.A., Mr. Fletcher."

"Um. Would you mind spelling that?"

Coming into the cool dark of the living room, blinded by the sun on the beach, Fletch had smelled cigar smoke and slowed at the French doors.

There were two forms, of men, sprawled on his living room furniture, one in the middle of the divan, the other on a chair.

"The Central Intelligence Agency," one of the forms muttered.

Fletch's bare feet crossed the marble floor to the carpet.

The style is perfect for the content. Now, let's apply the same style to a category romance novel about a woman on vacation at Cape Cod.

Carol woke up early. She got out of bed, went down to the window, knelt down. She didn't think about it. She just did it. A half hour later she stood up.

A romance reader would not read a romance written like that. The style is wrong because, while content for the private detective reader is mostly action, content for the romance reader is largely feelings. The romance reader wants to know what happens, but she also wants to know what it felt like.

So the form that Marian Chase used in *Share the Dream* is this:

Carol woke up early. The breeze from the sea floated through her open window, filling the room with a delicious freshness. For reasons that were more instinctive than thought out, Carol slipped out of the comforting bed and, still in her nightgown, knelt by the window for half an hour. With her chin resting on her hands and her elbows planted on the windowsill, Carol stared out at the rising sun, listening to the cawing of morning seagulls and the soothing clap-clap-clap of the waves rolling onto the beach.

An understanding of the relationship between form and content comes with writing a lot. Even an experienced editor or writer can't always say why form and content are incompatible, but he knows the conflict when he sees it or hears it. He knows that feeling of being tugged in two directions at the same time. And he knows that the damage done to a story by disharmony can rarely be repaired simply by writing another draft. Usually the writer must start over. So think about form and content before you write. Consider your material and your reader. Make your decisions about story type, length, format, slant, and style first. And then just write.

Closing Words

If you have finished reading this book and you're sitting there thinking, "Gee, there's more to it than I thought," then I have done my job. That's my point. There is more to it than you thought. There's more to it than any of us thought, and that goes double for the next person you meet at a party who has never written a word and says, "I could write a book." He can't. Maybe you can now, but he can't.

The techniques and principles you have just read about are advanced. They are the finer points of writing, and they are not the things you learn in a ten-week writing course. For the writer who has read *Make Every Word Count* or other beginner's books, they are usually the difference between getting published and getting rejected. I hope that if you are getting published now, that the things you have learned in this book will help you to get published more often and for larger paychecks. If you're not getting published, then I hope this book will help you to get published. If it does, keep in mind something I said in my introduction to *Make Every Word Count:*

"There is a difference between published and unpublished writers, but it is one of degree, not an absolute. Publication is not some magical turning point after which you suddenly know all there is to know about writing. It is more a measure of your progress along a path toward an imaginary point of writing perfection (which of course can never be reached)."

For myself, I hope that *Beyond Style* has been a measure of my progress toward that imaginary point of perfect writing. And for you I hope it has been, and will continue to be, a lantern that illuminates that path, and helps you move more quickly toward your own writing goals.

Index

Wed. April 14 is an important day for me. it's the day my life changed

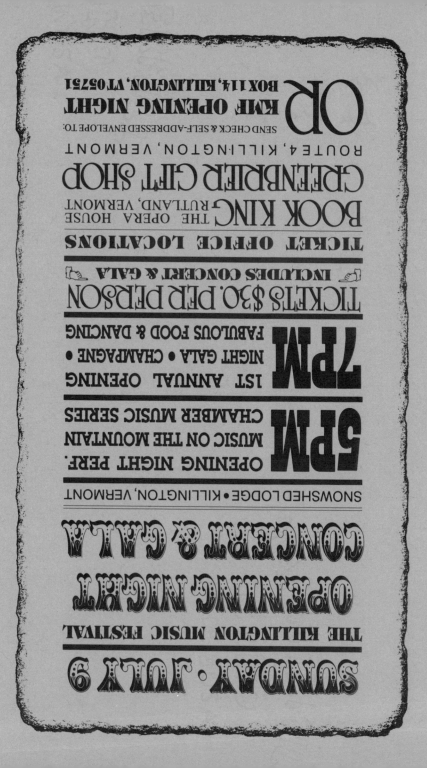

Other Books of Interest

Annual Market Books
    Artist's Market, edited by Susan Conner $18.95
    Children's Writer's & Illustrator's Market, edited by Connie Eidenier (paper) $14.95
    Novel & Short Story Writer's Market, edited by Laurie Henry (paper) $17.95
    Photographer's Market, edited by Connie Eidenier $19.95
    Poet's Market, by Judson Jerome $17.95
    Songwriter's Market, edited by Julie Whaley $17.95
    Writer's Market, edited by Glenda Neff $22.95

General Writing Books
    Beginning Writer's Answer Book, edited by Kirk Polking (paper) $12.95
    Beyond Style: Mastering the Finer Points of Writing, by Gary Provost $15.95
    How to Increase Your Word Power, by the editors of Reader's Digest $19.95
    How to Write a Book Proposal, by Michael Larsen $10.95
    Knowing Where to Look: The Ultimate Guide to Research, by Lois Horowitz (paper) $15.95
    Spider Spin Me a Web: Lawrence Block on Writing Fiction, by Lawrence Block $16.95
    12 Keys to Writing Books that Sell, by Kathleen Krull (paper) $12.95
    The 29 Most Common Writing Mistakes & How to Avoid Them, by Judy Delton $9.95
    Word Processing Secrets for Writers, by Michael A. Banks & Ansen Dibell (paper) $14.95
    The Writer's Digest Guide to Manuscript Formats, by Buchman & Groves $16.95

Nonfiction Writing
    How to Sell Every Magazine Article You Write, by Lisa Collier Cool (paper) $11.95
    The Writer's Digest Handbook of Magazine Article Writing, edited by Jean M. Fredette $15.95
    Writing Creative Nonfiction, by Theodore A. Rees Cheney $15.95

Fiction Writing
    The Art & Craft of Novel Writing, by Oakley Hall $16.95
    Characters & Viewpoint, by Orson Scott Card $12.95
    Dare to Be a Great Writer: 329 Keys to Powerful Fiction, by Leonard Bishop $15.95
    Dialogue, by Lewis Turco $12.95
    Fiction is Folks: How to Create Unforgettable Characters, by Robert Newton Peck (paper) $8.95
    Handbook of Short Story Writing: Vol 1, by Dickson and Smythe (paper) $9.95
    Handbook of Short Story Writing: Vol. II, edited by Jean M. Fredette $15.95
    One Great Way to Write Short Stories, by Ben Nyberg $14.95
    Plot, by Ansen Dibell $12.95
    Revision, by Kit Reed $13.95
    Writing the Modern Mystery, by Barbara Norville $15.95
    Writing the Novel: From Plot to Print, by Lawrence Block (paper) $9.95

Special Interest Writing Books
    Comedy Writing Secrets, by Melvin Helitzer $16.95
    The Complete Book of Scriptwriting, by J. Michael Straczynski (paper) $10.95
    Editing Your Newsletter, by Mark Beach (paper) $18.50
    Families Writing, by Peter Stillman (paper) $15.95
    How to Write Romances, by Phyllis Taylor Pianka $13.95
    How to Write Tales of Horror, Fantasy & Science Fiction, edited by J.N. Williamson $15.95
    How to Write & Sell Your Personal Experiences, by Lois Duncan (paper) $9.95
    How to Write Western Novels, by Matt Braun $13.95
    The Poet's Handbook, by Judson Jerome (paper) $9.95
    Successful Scriptwriting, by Jurgen Wolff & Kerry Cox $18.95

Writing for Children & Teenagers, 3rd Edition, by Lee Wyndham & Arnold Madison (paper) $12.95

The Writing Business

A Beginner's Guide to Getting Published, edited by Kirk Polking $11.95

The Complete Guide to Self-Publishing, by Tom & Marilyn Ross (paper) $16.95

How to Sell & Re-Sell Your Writing, by Duane Newcomb $11.95

How to Write Irresistible Query Letters, by Lisa Collier Cool $11.95

How to Write with a Collaborator, by Hal Bennett with Michael Larsen, $11.95

How You Can Make $25,000 a Year Writing (No Matter Where You Live), by Nancy Edmonds Hanson $15.95

Time Management for Writers, by Ted Schwarz $10.95

To order directly from the publisher, include $2.50 postage and handling for 1 book and 50¢ for each additional book. Allow 30 days for delivery.

Writer's Digest Books, 1507 Dana Avenue, Cincinnati, Ohio 45207
Credit card orders call TOLL-FREE
1-800-543-4644 (Outside Ohio)
1-800-551-0884 (Ohio only)
Prices subject to change without notice.

Write to this same address for information on *Writer's Digest* magazine, Writer's Digest Book Club, Writer's Digest School, and Writer's Digest Criticism Service.